Grade 5

BENCHMARK LITERACY™

Texts for Close Reading

Table of Contents

Unit 1

Table of Contents

Mutualism in Nature

Mutualism is the name for the relationship between two animal species in which both sides benefit. The two fish in the photograph—a grouper and a wrasse—have this type of relationship. How does mutualism work for the grouper and the wrasse?

When a wrasse comes upon a grouper, it does a little dance. This dance lets the bigger fish know it should slow down and open its mouth. The wrasse swims in and cleans the grouper's mouth and gills. The little fish gets a meal—quite a nice benefit! Then the wrasse swims away.

The grouper benefits also. The grouper now has a cleaner mouth and gills, which means less chance of disease for the bigger fish.

Energy Resources

We rely on nonrenewable and renewable resources for energy to light and heat our homes and run our cars.

Fossil fuels such as oil, natural gas, and coal are examples of nonrenewable resources, or resources that can't be replaced. Fossil fuels are the least expensive resources we have, but they can cause a great deal of pollution. Because fossil fuels are nonrenewable, some experts think we may run out of them in the future.

Solar power and wind power are examples of renewable resources, or resources that are constantly replaced. These resources do not pollute. And we aren't going to run out of sunshine or wind! But at this time, the technologies required to use solar power and wind power are very expensive.

Joseph Stalin

From 1929 until 1953, Joseph Stalin was dictator of the former Soviet Union, the largest country in the world. As dictator, Stalin ran the country as he wished, without asking for approval from others.

When Stalin became dictator, he took land from hundreds of thousand of farmers. He had the peasants who worked for the farmers murdered or sent to brutal labor camps. Stalin used the farmers' land to create huge farms owned by the government.

Many farmers defied Stalin by destroying crops and livestock. As punishment, Stalin had these farmers killed. From the late 1920s to the early 1930s, millions of farmers and peasants died as a result of Stalin's dictatorship.

Stalin believed that most people were his enemies. In the 1930s, he began the Great Purge. Stalin had about four million more people, whom he identified as enemies, murdered or put in prison.

The Great White Shark

The great white shark is the world's largest predatory shark. A full-grown great white shark can be 14 to 18 feet (4 to 5 meters) long. It can weigh up to 4,000 pounds (1,814 kilograms). A great white shark's jaw can open more than 3 feet (1 meter) wide. This allows the shark to handle large prey, such as seals and sea lions.

There are about 300 triangular-shaped teeth in rows inside a shark's mouth. Upper and bottom teeth work together on prey. Bottom teeth hold prey in place. Top teeth that are 3 inches (8 centimeters) long tear into flesh. A great white shark is constantly losing and growing new teeth.

The great white swims in coastal waters everywhere except for the polar regions. It has a powerful sense of smell, which allows it to detect even one drop of blood in the water.

The great white shark is considered the world's deadliest shark. It is able to overpower most people. But many scientists believe that great whites do not attack humans on purpose. Although the shark has excellent eyesight in dark seawater, things look blurry up close. Scientists think the sharks are mistaking people for seals and sea lions. There are only about 400 recorded attacks by great whites on humans, and most were not fatal.

Pirates

Pirates are thieves on the high seas. Real pirates are very different from the likable pirates in popular films. Pirates use weapons and force to take over ships. The ships have crews and may have valuable goods onboard. Pirates capture people and products and demand a ransom for their safe return.

In 2009, a band of pirates was working along the coast of Somalia. Somalia is in Africa. The Somali pirates took over a U.S. cargo ship and held the captain hostage. The U.S. Navy freed him by killing three pirates. The ship's crew began carrying weapons. When the same ship was attacked again, they were able to fight off the pirates. That failed attempt did not stop the pirates. Somali pirates continued to board ships of all nations and sometimes killed their hostages.

Pirates have a long history of violence. In the early 1700s, Blackbeard was the most violent. He worked off the coasts of the West Indies and the American colonies. He wore two swords at his waist. If he needed to use them, he did not waste any time.

Some historians say Blackbeard never killed anyone who did not try to kill him first. But in two years of pirating, Blackbeard was so bloodthirsty that today he is still considered the world's most notorious pirate.

This ship was one of more than sixty that were attacked by pirates near the Horn of Africa in 2009.

The Inuit Keep Their Traditions Alive

"Listen, children. Listen to the beat of the drum."

Inuit elder Sara Olanna starts to play a flat, caribou-skin drum. Her husband, Joseph, begins to dance. He is wearing a wooden mask painted to look like a seal. And though he is in his eighties, he moves gracefully. He moves just like a swimming seal. As he dances, Sara sings. Her song thanks the seal for its meat and fur.

It's a special day for the Inuit children in Tanalipaq (tah-NAH-lee-pahk) Public School. They are getting their first lesson in drum dancing. It's one of the oldest Inuit traditions, about 5,000 years old. People like Sara and Joseph want to keep Inuit traditions, and Joseph want to keep Inuit culture alive.

And the children are eager to learn. To them, it is a part of their past they have heard about only in stories. But today, that past is coming alive.

Like any modern-day people, the Inuit of the Canadian Yukon shop in stores and supermarkets. They use trucks, cars, powerboats, and snowmobiles to get around. They live in wood and concrete houses. They watch television and listen to the radio. They read books and use computers. But they also remember their past. They honor their history through dancing, singing, storytelling, and art.

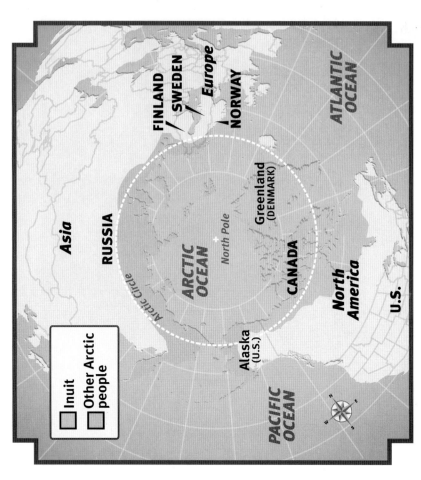

The Inuit people live in parts of Russia, Alaska, Canada, and Greenland.

Less than 100 years ago, the Inuit were still living the same way they had lived for centuries. Proud of their traditional ways, they had also given themselves the name "Inuit," which means "the people."

Long ago, the Inuit had learned how to survive in the harshest climate. They tamed wild dogs and used them to pull sleds through the snow. In the spring and summer, they lived by inland rivers, where they fished for salmon. They hunted deer and caribou. They picked berries. In the autumn, they traveled to the coast. They used kayaks and large canoes to hunt whales, walruses, and seals. They dried the meat and fish so that they could have food through the long, dark, winter months.

The Inuit would live in different houses, depending on the seasons. In the spring and summer, they lived in tents made of wooden poles covered with caribou and deer skins. In the autumn and winter, they lived in underground homes by the sea. The homes were covered with mossy dirt, or sod. They slept on wooden boards covered with sealskins. They wore seal fur clothes and boots. And when they went hunting for seals and polar bears out on the ice, they built temporary houses called igloos. The igloos were made out of large blocks of ice and had rounded, dome-like roofs. Tunnel-like doorways were made by cutting openings in the thick ice.

During the long winter from November to March, it was too dark and dangerous to hunt or fish. So the Inuit stayed inside. They spent the time sewing clothes and making hunting spears. They carved animals and made jewelry out of wood, metal, stone, and whalebone. They made painted wooden masks and animal-skin drums. And they told stories to the children. They told stories about how Earth was created. They told stories about past hunting adventures. The Inuit elders told the children tales about their ancestors. And the elders sang and danced.

Traditional Inuit drum dancers perform during a ceremony celebrating the creation of the Nunavut territory.

For thousands of years, the Inuit handed down their stories, songs, and dances to their children. And their children did the same thing. But in the 1800s and 1900s, the Inuit began to lose their connection with their culture. Christian missionaries, European fur traders, and American gold miners began to settle in the Yukon. They brought their own ways of life. Often, the Inuit were forced to give up their own language, traditions, and beliefs. Today, they still do some traditional hunting and fishing. But they also learned to hunt with guns, drive snowmobiles, and live in permanent houses.

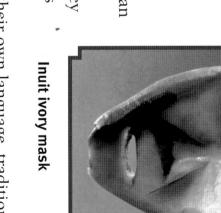

Inuit ivory mask

Fortunately, a movement has grown among the Inuit to reclaim their past. Inuit public school children learn their native language, Inuktitut (ih-NOOK-tih-toot), along with English. They hold ceremonies that celebrate the seasons. And, like the children of Tanalipaq, they learn from their elders how to drum dance.

"Now, children, you dance, too," says Joseph Olanna. He holds out his arms. One by one, the children join him as Sara beats the drum and sings. Once again, the Inuit culture's most glorious past will live on in the Inuit people's future.

	Inuit Life of Centuries Ago	Inuit Life Today
Homes	tents, sod houses, igloos	wooden and concrete houses
Food	walrus, whales, seals, deer, caribou, salmon, berries	some traditional foods, mostly supermarket foods
Transportation	dog sleds, kayaks, canoes	cars, trucks, snowmobiles, powerboats
Clothing	animal furs and skins	some animal furs, mostly modern clothes
Hunting Tools	wooden spears, knives	guns
Language(s)	Inuktitut	Inuktitut, English
Entertainment	stories, dances, songs	books, TV, radio, computers, traditional stories, dances, songs

This chart compares how the Inuit lived long ago with modern-day Inuit life.

Reread the Informational Text

Analyze the Information in the Text

- What is the text about?
- Why did the Inuit lose their connection with their culture?
- How did the Inuit of long ago change their lifestyles with the seasons?
- How does the text end?

Focus on Comprehension: Identify Main Idea and Supporting Details

- What is the main idea of the second paragraph in the text? What details support that main idea?
- Pages 10 and 11 are about how the Inuit adapted to their location. What details support this unstated main idea?
- What is the main idea for the second-to-last paragraph of the text? How does that main idea compare to the main idea of the whole text?
- What could be another good title for this text?

Analyze the Tools Writers Use: Text and Graphic Features

- What conclusion can you draw from the Inuit map on page 10?
- The author included a chart on page 12 that compares Inuit life long ago and today. What part of the text does this chart support?

Focus on Words: Superlatives

Make a chart like the one below. Locate each superlative in the text. Identify which word the superlative is describing.

Page	Superlative	What word is the superlative describing?
9	oldest	
10	harshest	
12	most glorious	

A True Team

The members of the Chariots softball team held a meeting to talk about buying uniforms. "The ones we have now are falling apart," Rob said.

"That's right," agreed Susan. "We need new uniforms so we'll look good when we win the title in August!"

"But how are we going to get the money?" asked John.

Over the next few weeks, members of the Chariots team could be seen all over town washing cars, cutting grass, and painting fences. The team members met again to decide which uniforms to buy with the $380 they had earned. Everyone was chattering and smiling. Susan noticed that Jed, who had worked the hardest, wasn't there.

"Where's Jed?" she asked.

"Didn't you hear?" replied John. "There was a fire at his house last night. The family is staying with friends until they can get their house fixed."

The team fell silent as the mood of the room changed. Finally, Rob spoke up, "You know, we've played every game in these uniforms. They've brought us good luck!"

"They sure have," said John. Everyone agreed with Rob and John. Two days later, Jed's family received a check for $380 in the mail.

One Giant Leap (Excerpt 1)

Amanda: Dad, are you still there? What did it feel like during liftoff? We were three miles away, and we felt the ground shake.

Mike Collins: It squashed us in our seats until we could barely breathe. It added "Gs," or gravitational forces. Right now, Amanda, you feel one G. On liftoff we felt three Gs. It was like being at the bottom curve of a roller coaster.

Todd: Cool!

Mission Control Expert 2: You need all that thrust at liftoff because the rocket is so heavy.

Amanda: But it weighs almost nothing in space, right?

Mission Control Expert 1: If your dad wanted to, he could push the ship with his hands.

Emma: That's pretty amazing, isn't it, Amanda?

Amanda: Mom, didn't you say Buzz and Neil won't weigh much on the moon?

Emma: Yes, I did, Amanda.

Mission Control Expert 2: Your mom's right. Another one of Newton's laws says that gravity attracts all masses to one another. And the greater the mass, the greater the gravity. The moon's mass is about 1/80 the mass of Earth. Its gravity is about one-sixth the gravity of Earth. On Earth, the two astronauts who will walk on the moon each weigh 360 pounds with their space suits on. On the Moon they weigh only 60—

Mission Control Expert 1: I'm sorry, but I have to interrupt you now. We have the lunar module on the line. Neil, what is your status?

Neil Armstrong: We're approaching the landing site. It looks pretty rocky. I'll keep moving to see if I can find a smoother spot.

15

One Giant Leap (Excerpt 2)

Emma: Todd, the most powerful telescope in the world couldn't see something as small as the *Columbia*. It's too far away.

Mission Control Expert 1: Your mom's right. Think of how far away your father is. His rocket goes 24,000 miles per hour, and it still took him two days to get to the moon.

Todd: My dad went 24,000 miles per hour?

Mission Control Expert 2: That's right. And do you know why? There's no air and very little gravity in space, so you can travel very fast. Newton's first law of motion states that once you are moving, you won't stop or change direction unless a force acts on you. In a car, friction with the ground constantly slows you down. In an airplane, air resistance works against forward motion. But in space there's nothing to stop you!

Todd: But because there's air and gravity on Earth, it took tons of fuel to lift off, right?

Mission Control Expert 1: Right. Remember, the rocket that launched this mission had three stages. The first stage had seven and one-half million pounds of thrust. That's a lot of power. The rocket pushed off the ground on a jet of superheated gas. The second stage needed less than half the power, because the rocket was lighter after all that fuel burned off. The third stage was the smallest, even though it carried the astronauts the farthest.

Todd: But if there's no air to push against in space, how does the rocket move forward?

Mission Control Expert 2: Good question. That's Newton's second law of motion—every action has an equal and opposite reaction. When the exhaust gases leave the rocket, they push back and the rocket moves forward. On liftoff, the force of the exhaust gases moving down propels the rocket in the opposite direction—up—with the same force.

Unit 2

Table of Contents

Measuring Weight

You use many different measuring tools when you do scientific experiments. You can use a spring scale to measure weight or the force of gravity on objects. Try this experiment that measures the weight of two stuffed animals.

Collect two different stuffed animals. Then hook the end of the spring scale to one of the animals and lift up the scale. As the force of gravity pulls the stuffed animal down, the spring scale stretches.

Record the weight showing on the spring scale. After you weigh the first stuffed animal, predict if the second stuffed animal will weigh more or less than the first. Weigh the second stuffed animal on the spring scale and record its weight.

Finally, compare the weight of the second animal to the weight of the first. Was your prediction correct or incorrect?

The *Titanic*

"Titanic" means huge. That was the perfect name for the gigantic ship named the *Titanic*. Construction on the Titanic began on March 31, 1909. More than 14,000 men worked for three years to build the huge ship. When the *Titanic* was completed in March 1912, it was the biggest ship of its time. It was as long as 2 ½ football fields and weighed almost 50,000 tons.

On April 12, 1912, about 2,200 passengers boarded the *Titanic* for its first voyage. The ship was sailing from England to New York City.

At 11:40 P.M. on April 14, the ship was a few hundred miles away from the coast of Canada. What happened next terrified passengers and crew. The *Titanic* struck an iceberg. Soon, water began to flood into the ship. The crew tried to evacuate passengers. But there were not enough lifeboats to hold everyone on board.

Then, at about 2:20 A.M. on April 15, the *Titanic* split in two and sank. More than 1,500 people died, most by drowning or freezing to death in the icy water.

Jim Bridger, Mountain Man

When Jim Bridger was eighteen years old, he answered a newspaper ad to join a beaver-trapping expedition. Jim traveled with the trappers more than 1,800 miles (2,897 kilometers) up the Missouri River to the Yellowstone River. On the trip, Jim learned to live in the wilderness. He became a mountain man.

Two years later, in 1824, Jim joined an expedition that explored the South Pass Trail across the Rocky Mountains. Soon, settlers headed for California began to use the South Pass Trail.

Many years later, in 1850, Bridger found a shorter route across the Rocky Mountains. He named this route Bridger Pass. Stagecoaches began to use Bridger Pass to cross the Rocky Mountains.

After finding Bridger Pass, Jim worked as a scout for the U.S. Army. But as he got older, Bridger began to go blind, and he retired from his job as an army scout. In 1867, he bought a farm in Missouri. He died on his farm in 1881. He was seventy-seven years old.

A Disastrous Dog-Walking Day

Courtney loved dogs so much that she had decided to become a veterinarian when she grew up. For now, she was content to be her neighborhood's most sought-after dog walker.

Every day after school, Courtney walked several dogs together in the park. First she picked up Milo, the dachshund, and then she got two terriers, Mabel and Marla. Last, she got Rodney, a beagle who enjoyed barking loudly.

Today Milo went left when Mabel went right. Marla didn't want to walk at all, and Rodney barked and barked. This is a disaster, thought Courtney.

Finally, she got all the dogs walking together, and then she returned them to their homes. But she couldn't find the key to Rodney's apartment. Rodney barked relentlessly until she found the key.

Now Courtney had to pick up Dudley, a dog she had never walked before. Dudley tugged on his leash all the way to the park.

Dudley suddenly pulled Courtney over to a man eating an ice cream cone. Dudley jumped up and licked the cone, while Courtney tried to pull him off.

The man was laughing, though, because it turned out he and Dudley knew each other! "Let me get some ice cream for us all!" he said. What a sweet ending to Courtney's disastrous dog-walking day!

Here, Kitty-Kitty!

It wasn't that Jamal didn't like cats, but Kitty could be a major pain. When he was doing his homework, she sat on his papers and batted at his pen. When he was playing his digital games, she sometimes stepped on a key, ruining the game.

"Haven't you heard that cats aren't supposed to be so friendly?" said Jamal. Kitty just purred.

One day after school, Jamal spread out his homework. He was deep into solving math problems when he realized that something was wrong. Kitty wasn't sprawled across the papers.

Kitty didn't appear at dinnertime, and she wasn't around when Jamal played Space Cruisers. Kitty had disappeared and Jamal was really worried.

"Here, Kitty-Kitty," he called, but when no cat came purring, the whole family began to search for her. First they looked in all the bedrooms, and then they looked in the basement. Finally, Jamal heard muffled meowing coming from the laundry room.

He opened the door and out came Kitty! "She must have gotten locked in when I did the wash this morning," said Jamal's mother.

"Come on, Kitty," said Jamal, relieved and happy to see his friend. "You need to go over—I mean, roll over—my English homework!"

Linda's Journal

I was there because I was determined to become a great writer. A great writer needs a cool, quiet, private place to work, and the cave was perfect on this sizzling hot day.

Okay, I'll admit it. I was trying to write as well as Maria. Everyone is always saying that Maria is a brilliant writer, so I guess she is, although I'm not sure I like the way she describes flowers and sunsets and things. True, she does make up clever stories and twisting plots and thrilling adventures, but I was pretty sure I could write better stories if I had a quiet place to concentrate.

No one seemed to be around, so I moved closer to the entrance of the cave, leaned against the cool wall, and tried to think of something exciting to write about. I flipped through my new journal and read the fragments I'd jotted down. There were words like "missing seagull" and "buried copper penny—found again," but they didn't spark any adventure story ideas.

"Linda! Hey, LINDA! It's basketball time!" My brother Jake sounded impatient and a little peeved, but I didn't care. There was something I needed to do and it had nothing to do with basketball.

I moved a little farther into the cave so he wouldn't see me if he decided to look down at this end of the beach. I didn't go in too far because I'm afraid of the dark shadowy corners where the light from the entrance doesn't reach.

Jake kept shouting my name, and I couldn't think of anything to write about, so I decided to take a break. I ripped out a few empty pages and stuffed them into the back pocket of my jeans, along with my little pencil. Then I shoved my journal into a high crevice where no one would find it and raced down the hill to find my brother.

"I'm the greatest player on the planet!" Jake was saying, just like he always does. "No one can ever beat me." *Swish!* "Another perfect shot! Call in the professional scouts 'cause Jake the Great is ready for the big time!"

"You're not that good, Jake!" I hollered as I stomped away. "I'm going to find something to write about, and it isn't your basketball nonprowess!"

Cai and his dog Tucker were swinging in the hammock that his grandmother had hung on her porch the day before.

I hid behind the maple tree next to the porch, pulled the pencil and paper out of my back pocket, and watched them. Cai was cradling a ragged baby-blue stuffed bunny and talking to Tucker.

"You're the only one I can talk to about this because it's a secret, and you can't tell anyone because you're a dog. It's so embarrassing," Cai said.

I moved a little closer and waited for Cai to blurt out his secret. It took a few minutes, but he finally said it. "No one else in the whole world knows that I still can't fall asleep without this old baby toy with me. I should get rid of Jumper but I really don't want to."

Tucker said, "Woof," licked Cai's face, and snuggled up beside him. After a while they both fell asleep, so I wrote Cai's words on my paper and tiptoed away. Cai's problem wasn't exactly an adventure story, but a big kid who can't give up his baby toy was much more interesting than anything I'd thought of.

When I was finished jotting down some notes I went home for a glass of water. Jake was still shooting hoops, but he had stopped bragging. He was mumbling to himself something that I couldn't quite hear, so I skipped the water and snuck up behind him to listen.

"I'm a fraud," Jake was muttering. "Sure, I can score points against my sister, but who can't? She's a lousy guard, but I'm not really that good. Mediocre is what I am, and I'll never make the team when I get to high school."

"Fraud. Mediocre. Lousy guard." I wrote the words so I wouldn't forget what Jake had said. I couldn't wait to write a story about somebody who acts like he's the best but really isn't sure if he is. I'll bet Maria had never thought of a story as good as that.

Maria's kitchen window was wide open, and she was sitting at the table, writing in her journal. I had been standing outside the window for a few minutes, trying to decide if I should interrupt her, when her mother called, "Time to come up and get ready for the restaurant, Maria!"

When Maria ran upstairs, I climbed in the window and read the page she'd been working on. It was a story about a tiny boat that got caught in a storm. I copied seven words that would help me remember what Maria's story was about.

"Tranquil, smog, gusty, nausea, howling, ferocious, terrified."

Click click click. The sound of Maria's mother's high heels were heading toward the stairs. "Ready to go to eat?" she asked.

I didn't wait to hear if Maria was ready or not. I just beat it out of there and *whoosh!*—raced straight up to the cave so that I could transfer my notes to my journal before I forgot everything I'd heard.

I couldn't think of how to end my story, so I hid my journal in the crevice and left the cave.

The next morning my parents put together a fancy brunch for people new to the beach. I decided to hang around and splurge by wolfing down two pastries, but there was so much "Hello. How do you do? I'm Linda" happening that I never got around to eating them. I put the pastries in a baggie and carried them up to the cave to eat later when I needed a delicious break from writing in my journal. I went straight to the crevice, reached up, and felt around.

My journal was gone!

I was still searching when I heard Tucker's bark leading Cai, Maria, and Jake toward the cave. I hid in a dark corner and waited. They were inside now, standing together near the entrance where I could see them. Cai was holding my journal.

"Tucker and I were in the cave early this morning," he said. "I happened to look up and saw something sticking out of that crevice."

This is what I wrote:

☐ *Once upon a time, there was a boy who was embarrassed because he still sleeps with his baby toy Jumper. He had a friend who bragged about being a great basketball player, but this friend was really a fraud. Deep down he thought that he was a mediocre player who could score only against lousy guards like his sister. This boy was the only person in the whole world who thought his sister was lousy, but that's another story.*

☐ *One day the two friends went out in a tiny boat. At first the day was tranquil.*

☐ *There was a small amount of smog in the air, but not much. After a while the wind grew gusty and nausea set in. The wind was howling, the sky was ferocious, the friends were terrified.*

☐

☐

☐

☐

"Can you believe what she wrote?" Maria said. "She must have read my journal. That's invading my privacy."

"Your privacy!" Jake squawked. "She was listening in on me talking to my private self."

"She must have been hiding behind the maple tree, listening to me telling Tucker my secret," Cai said. "What a terrible thing to do."

My heart was really beating hard now. If I didn't get out of that cave soon I'd faint or die or even worse—get killed by my friends.

And then it happened! I must have breathed really, really hard because they all turned at once. They came over, surrounded me, and glared down.

"Aren't journals private?" I said hopefully. "You really shouldn't be reading someone else's journal."

"You can say that again," Maria said.

"Thoughts are private, too!" Jake hissed.

Cai didn't say anything, but Maria did. "Don't be embarrassed, Cai. Everyone worries about something. I still sleep with a night-light."

Maria opened my journal and started to write. When she was finished, she slid it into my no-longer-secret crevice and led the others out of the cave.

When they were gone, I retrieved my journal and read what she had written.

I signed my name and was about to leave the cave when I realized that something miraculous had occurred—besides me learning a valuable lesson. So much had happened in the cave that I wasn't afraid of being in there in the dark. I was over my fear!

Cai and Maria and Jake were waiting right outside, and it was obvious they'd been watching to see if I signed. The day was cooler and it looked like rain. "Anybody hungry?" I held up the pastries and everybody nodded. I broke the pastries in half and we each had a piece.

LINDA's Secrets

I promise that I will never ever again eavesdrop on my friends. I will not sneak into their houses or hide behind trees to spy on them.

I promise that I will never use my friends' secrets in my writing again.

Signed _____.
    [Sign your name here.]

Reread the Story

Analyze the Characters, Setting, and Plot

- Who are the main characters in this story?
- Why is Linda in the cave?
- What is Linda's problem?
- Linda finds out some interesting things about Cai, Jake, and Maria. How does she find out these things?
- What happens at the end of the story?

Focus on Comprehension: Summarize Information

- Write a one-sentence summary for each of the four children in this story, identifying their problems.
- In one sentence, summarize the oath that Linda signs.
- In one sentence, summarize how Linda overcame her fear.

Focus on Motif

Authors often using recurring themes, or ideas, in stories. Recurring themes are called motifs. What is the motif for this story?

Analyze the Tools Writers Use: Onomatopoeia

- On page 24, Jake says "swish." What sound is the author trying to describe with that word? Is this a loud or soft sound?

- On page 25, the dog says "woof." Why does the author use onomatopoeia in this part of the story? What do you think the dog is saying? How can you tell?
- On page 25, the author says that Maria's mother's high-heeled shoes were making a click-click-click sound. What part of the shoes is making the sound?
- On page 25, the author says that Linda made a whoosh sound as she traveled to the cave. Is Linda moving quickly or slowly? How can you tell?

Focus on Words: Portmanteau Words

Make a chart like the one below. For each portmanteau word, write its definition. Then identify the two words that make up the portmanteau word.

Page	Word	Definition	Word Is Made From
24	blurt		
25	smog		
26	brunch		
26	splurge		
27	squawked		

Symbols

A symbol is something that stands for something else. For example, numerals are symbols; they stand for exact amounts of things. Letters are symbols, too; they stand for sounds.

There are many symbols that stand for ideas, such as the symbols that stand for the United States: the flag, Uncle Sam, and the bald eagle. Scales represent justice; a dove represents peace.

Animals are often used as symbols. Ants and bees symbolize industriousness. The fox symbolizes cleverness. The owl symbolizes wisdom.

You are familiar with color-coded symbols, such as red, yellow, and green traffic lights; red stop signs; and yellow warning signs. A clock . . . an hourglass . . . "Father Time" . . . these are all symbols of passing time.

Did you know that music uses symbols? The half-note . . . the quarter-note . . . the staff that the notes appear on . . . they are used to represent the sounds, or notes, that make up a song.

There are many symbols—thousands of them—that you use every day without thinking about them. In fact, you've been using symbols on this poster. They're called punctuation marks!

Tornado! (Excerpt 1)

Laurie: Hey, Douglas, where are Mom and Dad? Douglas? Douglas! Will you please pause that video game and listen to me?

Douglas: What?

Laurie: Do you know where Mom and Dad are? They're supposed to take Jazz and me to our soccer game.

Douglas: They went to the grocery store, but they said they'd be right back.

Jazz: The game doesn't start for another hour and a half, Laurie, so there's plenty of time. We can spray-paint our hair green to match our uniforms. And I've got green nail polish in my bag. Let's paint our fingernails green, too! That way our uniforms, socks, cleats, hair, and nails will all be green, and we'll look totally fearsome! The other team will freak out when they see us running onto the field.

Laurie: Okay, let's do our nails first, so they'll be dry before the game. Douglas, will you tell us when Mom and Dad get here? Douglas! Oh, never mind, here come Aaron and Ike. Hey, Aaron, let us know when Mom and Dad come back because they have to take us to our game.

Aaron: Um, you may not have noticed, but it's going to rain. Take a look outside; the sky is black. That's why we came in.

Jazz: I hope our game doesn't get canceled.

Ike: The wind's starting to pick up, too.

Jazz: Whoa! Look at the trees in the neighbor's yard. They're really getting blown around! But it's not raining yet, so maybe our game is still on.

Tornado! (Excerpt 2)

Ike: Did you say a measly little F-0 tornado caused all this damage? You've got to be kidding.

Laurie: That was Dad on the phone. He and Mom took shelter during the storm, and now they're on their way home. They said not to go outside until they get back, in case any power lines are down.

Ike: That's fine with me because there's no way I'm setting foot outside this house.

Jazz: Well, the soccer game is definitely going to be canceled, or at least postponed. I'm just going to call my mom and tell her I'm okay.

Aaron: Ike, aren't your parents supposed to pick you up at 3:45? It's not even 3:00 yet. Can you believe we were in that bathroom for less than twenty minutes?

Laurie: And Ike thought it was a gazillion centuries. Time sure doesn't fly when you're frightened, huh, Ike?

Ike: Okay, I admit it: I was frightened. And I apologize for making fun of you earlier, Douglas.

Douglas: That's okay. The main thing is, we're all safe.

Ike: Do you think you could show me how to play that puzzle video game?

Laurie: I thought you said that was a nerdly video game, Ike.

Ike: "Nerdly" isn't a word, Laurie. And nobody is calling my buddy Douglas a nerd ever again. From now on, he gets treated with respect because this future meteorologist has nerves of steel!

The End

Unit 3

Table of Contents

From *Treasure Island*

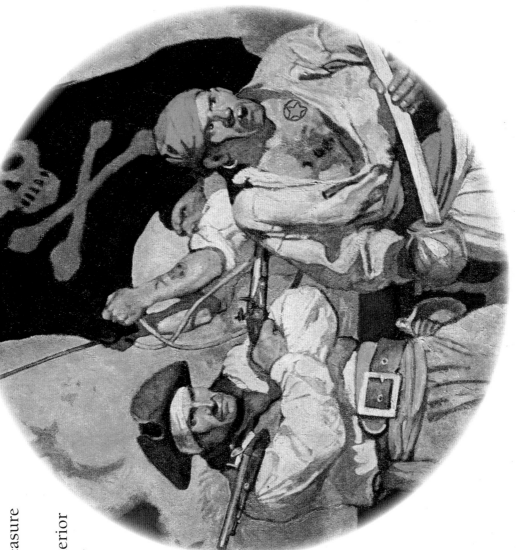

The following paragraphs are from the novel Treasure Island *by Robert Louis Stevenson.*

The red glare of the torch, lighting up the interior of the block house, shewed me the worst of my apprehensions realized. The pirates were in possession of the house and stores: there was the cask of cognac, there were the pork and bread, as before, and what tenfold increased my horror, not a sign of any prisoner. I could only judge that all had perished, and my heart smote me sorely that I had not been there to perish with them.

There were six of the buccaneers [pirates] all told; not another man was left alive. The parrot sat, preening her plumage, on Long John's shoulder. "So," said he, "here's Jim Hawkins, shiver my timbers! Dropped in, like eh? Well, come, I take that friendly."

Stars

In ancient times, stars were a mystery. People watched them form patterns and move across the night sky. Some ancient people made up stories about how the stars got in the sky. These people believed the stars were once people, gods, and goddesses.

Today, astronomers study the stars and help us understand them. We now know that stars are giant balls of gas that give off light and heat. We know that stars gather in groups called galaxies, and that galaxies can hold between ten million and one trillion stars. We also know how stars are formed, and how they fade from the sky.

Climbing Mount Everest

Reaching the peak of Mount Everest is not easy. Climbers face bitter cold winds while trekking through heavy snow. Deep crevasses in the ice open and close all the time, making the climb very dangerous.

Then there is the blowing snow, which makes it difficult to see. Powerful winds have actually blown climbers right off the mountainside. Avalanches, moving at speeds of 200 miles per hour (322 kilometers per hour), are the biggest killers of all.

At the top of Everest, there is only one-third as much oxygen as at sea level. Most, but not all, climbers need extra oxygen.

Upon reaching the summit, climbers can stay for only a few moments. If they stay longer, the lack of oxygen can weaken them, making the trek down difficult.

The Arrest of Susan B. Anthony

The deputy marshal of Rochester, New York, stood in the family parlor and asked to see Susan B. Anthony. Ten-year-old Clara Stafford watched as he arrested her aunt.

Four days earlier, Clara had listened, proud and shocked, when Aunt Susan said she had just cast her ballot in the election of 1872. Some of Clara's other aunts had voted with Susan. It made no sense to the Anthony family that men and women did not have equal rights. But according to the law, women did not have the right to vote. Aunt Susan's vote was illegal. Aunt Susan and the other women who belonged to the suffragist movement believed the law needed to change. Nothing in the Constitution, they insisted, denied them the right to vote.

Clara often heard her aunt speak about the need for women's rights. She was thrilled to have such a passionate aunt. She knew it was important for her own future. But right now, Clara was frightened.

Aunt Susan was very calm. She smiled at Clara and said she would be back soon. "Cautious, careful people," she said, "can never bring about a reform." When news of her arrest spread, she added, it would help to advance the suffragist cause. She kissed her niece and left the house. Clara hoped that someday she could be half as brave as her strong-minded, dedicated aunt.

On the Bus with Rosa Parks

One evening in 1955, I was headed home from downtown Montgomery, Alabama. I was standing in the back of the jostling bus, struggling to hold on and not drop the fresh apple pie that my Aunt Mavis had given me for my mama.

There were plenty of seats up front, but they were in the "Whites Only" section.

Soon, there wasn't an empty seat on the bus, and one white man was still standing. The bus driver yelled at the folks sitting in the first row of the colored section and insisted they get up. There was nothing abnormal about that, but what happened next I will remember my whole life.

One woman who appeared to be about my mama's age politely but firmly refused to get up. The driver threatened to call the police. To my surprise, the woman, who I later found out was named Mrs. Rosa Parks, remained seated.

Two policemen came to arrest Mrs. Parks. I heard her ask one of them, "Why do you push us around?" He replied, "I don't know. But the law is the law." They escorted Mrs. Parks off the bus. I couldn't say why, but I was sure I had just seen something really important take place.

Monitor vs. *Merrimack*: Clash of the Ironclads

W ill Randall stood on the deck of a strange boat, bundled up against the frigid winter air blowing off the icy water of New York Harbor. The tall, light-haired young man wore a heavy navy blue coat and thick woolen gloves, complemented by a naval cap. But the freezing, raw February weather could not dampen his enthusiasm and excitement. He was a first-time sailor on the newest, most up-to-date ship in the Union Navy.

The ship, an ironclad named the *Monitor*, had just departed from the Brooklyn Navy Yard. The vessel and its crew of more than fifty seamen were heading into enemy waters, in Virginia. When they arrived at Hampton Roads Harbor, the *Monitor* would take on ships of the Confederate States of America.

Will was proud to be a crewman on the *Monitor*. Cannonballs would just bounce off the iron-covered sides of this modern warship. As a gunner, he was looking forward to firing one of the ship's two very big guns.

But the enthusiasm Will and his crewmates were feeling quickly turned to frustration. This was the *Monitor's* maiden voyage and a mechanical problem appeared. The ship's helmsman discovered that the steering wasn't working well. It was stiff, making it very difficult to turn the ship.

A frustrated John Worden, the bearded captain of the *Monitor*, gave the order to return to port. Will and his fellow sailors were disappointed the *Monitor* hadn't gotten any farther than New York Harbor. People on shore laughed at the funny-looking, pancake-flat boat being towed back to the navy yard for repairs.

Hundreds of miles to the south, the navy of the Confederate States of America was completing an iron-covered ship of its own. Eli Reynolds, a dark-haired and muscular sailor, was helping to put the finishing touches on the South's first ironclad.

Eli was eager to get the new warship into action. Union ships had set up a blockade of the Virginian coastline, preventing supplies from getting through. The Confederate ship was going to break up the blockade. *We'll teach those Yankees a lesson,* Eli thought, as he helped push and fasten into place one of the ship's many big guns.

Following repairs and a two-day journey, the *Monitor* arrived at Virginia late on Saturday as the sky grew dark. Bad news awaited Captain Worden. That very day the *Merrimack* had attacked Union ships blockading the Virginian coastline. Using its ram and guns, the *Merrimack* had destroyed and set aflame two Union warships. It also seriously damaged a third ship, the *Minnesota.*

In addition to iron sides and a steam engine, the *Monitor* also had a gun turret on its deck. The turret was a circular room covered in iron, and it contained two cannons. Like a merry-go-round, the turret could be turned completely around so that the big guns could fire in any direction.

The South's ironclad was built using the bottom portion and steam engines of a Union ship, the *Merrimack*, which had been sunk in the harbor at Norfolk, Virginia. A new deck was put atop the *Merrimack's* hull, on which workers erected a huge, long cabin that would hold the ship's guns, including ten cannons, five on each side. To make the *Merrimack* deadlier, Confederate shipbuilders added a ram, a large, heavy point of iron, at the front of the ship. The ram would be used to poke large holes in enemy vessels to sink them. The new Confederate ironclad was given a new name, the *Virginia*, but most people still called the boat the *Merrimack*.

Hundreds of Union sailors lost their lives in that battle. Only the approaching darkness of night had stopped the *Merrimack* from doing more damage. In the distance, Captain Worden could see the smoke and red glow of the burning Union ships. He knew that if the *Merrimack* wasn't stopped, the next day it would attack and sink more Union vessels.

That evening, Captain Worden called the entire crew onto the deck of the *Monitor*. He pointed to the distant flames lighting up the night sky and told his men about the *Merrimack's* victory and the terrible loss of Union sailors and boats. He also said that the *Monitor* had just received orders to sail up to Washington, D.C., so that government officials could inspect the new ship.

"We have a choice, men," Captain Worden announced. "We can sail away to Washington to show off our boat, as instructed, or we can stay here and fight the *Merrimack* in the morning. We're all new to the *Monitor* and still learning the ropes. Further, for most of you, this would be your first naval combat. When the fighting begins, we'd run the risk of floundering," he explained. "In other words, men, we can't be sure we will win a fight with the *Merrimack*. So what do you think we ought to do? Should we follow our orders and leave here, or stay and fight?"

The officers and crew of the *Monitor* numbered more than fifty, but not one said a thing or offered an opinion. A cool breeze flapped the uniforms of the men as they stood in an uneasy silence. After a few long minutes, Will Randall spoke up.

"Captain, we didn't come all this way to turn around just when things get tough," he said. "I believe in the *Monitor* and I believe in the Union, and I say let's show those Rebels what *our* ironclad can do!"

The crew erupted into a great cheer in unison. Captain Worden gladly shook Will's hand. The rest of the men crowded around Will, thanking him and slapping him on the back. Will grinned and blushed. He was not used to being complimented.

A courageous decision had been made. The *Monitor* would stay and do battle to stop the destruction being caused by the Confederate ironclad.

At dawn on the morning of March 9, 1862, the *Merrimack* sailed out of Norfolk harbor again to attack and destroy more of the Union fleet. Eli Reynolds peered out through one of the warship's gun ports to see which Union ship Captain Catesby Jones would choose as the next victim of the *Merrimack*.

"Nobody can touch us," he said to himself. "Today, we'll finish the job we started yesterday."

Eli prepared to fire his cannon as the *Merrimack* approached its target, the damaged, unmoving *Minnesota*. She was a sitting duck.

To his surprise, Eli spotted a strange, flat, metal-covered boat coming out from behind the *Minnesota*. Another ironclad! Eli ran to the *Merrimack*'s captain to give him the news of the approaching vessel.

"I've never seen anything like it," Eli said. "It looks like a tin can on a metal raft."

"That must be the *Monitor* we've been hearing about," Captain Jones replied. "Well, Seaman Reynolds, it looks like we're in for a battle. Get back to your gun."

Eli aimed his cannon at the *Monitor* and fired. The shot missed, kicking up a big splash of water. The turret of the *Monitor* turned toward the *Merrimack*. Inside, Will Randall fired one of the two turret cannons. The eleven-inch-wide cannonball hit the *Merrimack* hard on the side. Union sailors aboard the foundering *Minnesota* cheered.

The *Monitor's* cannonball did not break through the protective iron plating of the *Merrimack*, but the loud bang and vibration caused Eli's nose to bleed. Eli wiped his bloody nose with his sleeve. There was no time to stop.

Captain Jones ordered the *Merrimack's* helmsman to turn the warship's side toward the *Monitor*, enabling the *Merrimack* to fire broadside from all the guns on one side of the ship. The *Merrimack* fired. The multiple shots dented the armor of the *Monitor* and rattled Will's teeth. But no serious harm had been done.

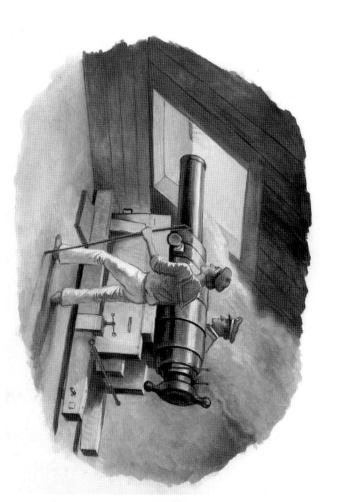

Like two prizefighters in a boxing match, the two ironclads circled each other, firing away. The *Monitor*, smaller than the *Merrimack*, was a bit quicker. Cannonballs rocketed and ricocheted off each ship. Clouds of gunpowder smoke surrounded the battling boats, making it hard for the crew of the *Minnesota* and the spectators on land to see what was happening.

After hours of exchanging shots, the *Merrimack's* captain decided to try ramming the *Monitor*. His helmsman aimed the front of the *Merrimack* at the *Monitor*. "Full speed!" Captain Jones ordered.

43

Because the *Monitor* was faster, Captain Worden managed to move his ship out of the path of the *Merrimack*, which struck the *Monitor* only a glancing blow. The *Monitor* suffered no damage, but, ironically, the minimal contact caused the *Merrimack* to spring a leak. The Confederate ironclad began taking on water. In need of repairs after three hours of artillery give and take, the *Merrimack* had to break off the fight.

As the *Merrimack* sailed away, Eli, his shirt covered with blood, sweat, and gunpowder soot, fired one last time at the *Monitor*, which was following the *Merrimack*. "Right into the pilot house!" he cried. "Wahoo!"

The *Merrimack*'s blast wounded the *Monitor*'s captain. Will rushed to kneel beside his fallen commander. As Will helped Captain Worden to the ship's medic for treatment, the captain ordered the *Monitor* to give up its pursuit of the *Merrimack*. The battle was now over as both ships headed off for repair.

Will Randall stepped into the damaged pilothouse and looked out the view hole. He watched the *Merrimack* move toward port. Both crews had fought courageously. This was the end of today's battle, Will knew, but the beginning of a new kind of naval warfare.

As Will observed the retreating *Merrimack*, he thought he saw, for a moment, a young, dark-haired sailor on the Confederate ironclad salute him. Will stood up tall and saluted back.

Reread the Story

Analyze the Characters, Setting, and Plot

- Who are the characters in this story?
- What is the setting for this story?
- What is the name of the Union ironclad? What is the name of the Confederate ironclad?
- What are the ironclads capable of doing?
- What is the problem with the *Monitor*? What did the sailors decide to do about the problem?
- The *Merrimack* captain decides to ram the *Monitor*. Why?
- What happens at the end of the story?

Focus on Comprehension: Make Inferences

- The author says that "cannonballs would just bounce off the iron-covered sides of this modern warship." What can you infer about the *Monitor* from this sentence?
- The *Merrimack* cannot do battle at night. How can you tell?
- The two young sailors on the ironclads have a mutual respect for each other. How can you tell?

Analyze the Tools Writers Use: A Strong Lead

Look at the lead in this story.

- What type of lead does the author use in this story?
- Did the lead hook you as a reader? Why?
- What did you expect to learn after reading the lead?

Focus on Words: Easily Confused Words

Make a chart like the one below. Locate the easily confused word in the story. Read the sentence containing each word and the sentences around it. Then write a definition for the word.

Page	Word	Definition
39	complemented	
42	complimented	
40	farther	
41	further	
41	floundering	
43	foundering	

The Way to Play the Game

Announcer 1: Welcome back to the championship game between Lincoln School and Crane School! This has been the most exciting basketball game I've ever seen. Wouldn't you agree?

Announcer 2: I would indeed! There are actually two competitions going on tonight. Kelly and Kathy Strong, twin sisters and Lincoln School's two best players, are also competing against each other for the most points scored in the season. Can you say "sibling rivalry"?

Announcer 1: Both players and both teams have been evenly matched throughout this game. Now, with seven seconds left to play, Crane and Lincoln are tied at 74 points, and Kelly is one point ahead of Kathy. Crane has the ball.

Announcer 2: No, Kathy Strong has stolen the ball! She is racing down the floor! She is on her way to the championship and the record!

Announcer 1: But Crane's Hodges and Benson are between Kathy Strong and the basket. Will she try for three points from that distance? But, wait, Kelly Strong is in a good position under the basket. What will Kathy do?

Announcer 2: Kathy fakes a jump shot and fires the ball to Kelly! Kelly makes the easy layup! Lincoln wins the championship, and Kelly gets the record! Now that's the way to play.

Ponce de Leon and the Fountain of Youth

(Excerpt 1)

Narrator: We're at the Conquistador Travel and Trade Show in Saint Augustine, Florida. It is a celebration of the early 1500s, when European explorers first came to the Americas. A visitor strolls past booths filled with artifacts from this era. The visitor stops to talk to one of the actors dressed as a Spanish explorer.

Randi: Excuse me, but what is a conquistador?

Cortés: *Conquistador* is a Spanish word that means "conqueror" or "explorer" or "adventurer." Like me— Hernán Cortés—at your service.

Randi: I've heard about you. You conquered what's called Mexico today. And destroyed the mighty Aztec empire in the process.

Cortés: It's true that the Spanish conquistadors killed lots of Aztecs and other native peoples with their guns. Unfortunately, the Europeans also brought deadly diseases with them to the New World. These diseases killed even more natives.

Randi: Diseases?

Cortés: Such as smallpox. The Aztecs and other natives had no way to fight these foreign diseases. They had not built up any natural immunity.

Randi: And they didn't have medicines like we do today.

Cortés: They caught the diseases, got sick, and died. Too bad they never found the "Fountain of Youth" that my fellow Spanish explorer, Ponce de Leon, spent years searching for.

Narrator: The visitor spots a huge banner over another booth and reads it.

Randi: "Juan Ponce de Leon and the Search for the Fountain of Youth." That sounds interesting.

Ponce de Leon and the Fountain of Youth
(Excerpt 2)

Ponce: Maybe not, but it is so beautiful. Such lush vegetation. Such wonderful beaches. What a wonderful place for theme parks. What's today's date, Diego?

Diego: It's Easter Sunday. Or, as we say in Spanish, Pascua de Flores. Easter of Flowers.

Ponce: Then I shall call this place Florida, in honor of this day of flowers. And I claim this island in the name of Spain.

Diego: Excellent name choice. Only Florida is not an island. It's a peninsula.

Ponce: Maybe so, Diego, but I can't spell peninsula. Come. Let us look for the Fountain.

Narrator: Ponce de Leon becomes the first European to set foot in Florida, near the city called Saint Augustine today. But he found no Fountain of Youth. Still hopeful, he set out to sea again. And for eight long years he continued to search and search and search—all in vain.

Diego: Ponce, for eight years we have explored the forests. We have looked through the fields. We have searched the shore. We have found giant turtles. We have found powerful ocean currents. We have found that the climate, though often hot and humid, could be nice when you get to retirement age. But we have not found the Fountain of Youth.

Ponce: In our search for eternal youth, we have both grown old, Diego.

Narrator: Ponce, now white-haired and almost broke, decides to search for the fabled fountain one last time in southern Florida.

Diego: The Indians here don't look as friendly as in Puerto Rico, Ponce. They're armed with spears, and bows and arrows.

Unit 4

Table of Contents

Horatio at the Bridge

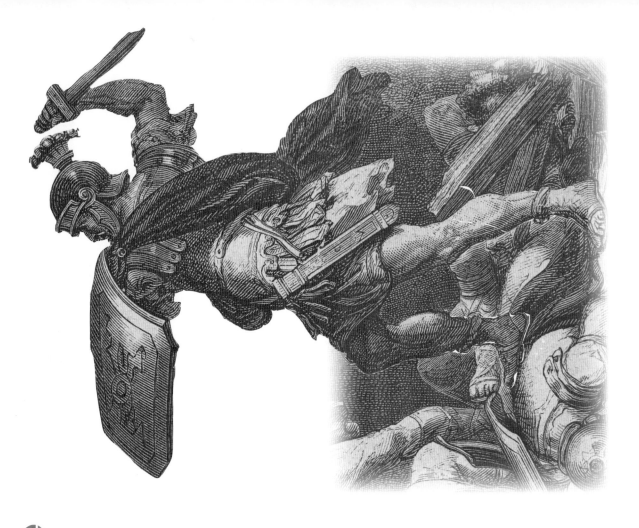

Around 800 B.C., people living near the Tiber River, in what is now Italy, joined to form the town of Rome. About 600 B.C., people known as Etruscans began to rule ancient Rome. A legend tells this story about the last Etruscan king and a Roman soldier named Horatio.

After nearly 100 years of Etruscan rule, the Romans drove the last Etruscan king out of their city. In anger, the king called on his army to attack Rome.

To reach Rome, the army had to cross a wooden bridge that spanned the Tiber River. When the Etruscans arrived at the bridge, Horatio was blocking the way. Alone, he fought off the enemy soldiers.

As Horatio fought, more Roman soldiers behind him ripped the bridge apart so the Etruscan army could not enter Rome.

When the last plank of the bridge fell, Horatio leapt into the river and swam to Rome. The Etruscan army did not get into the city.

Predator and Prey

A lynx is a kind of wild cat that chases hare or rabbits to eat them. The lynx is a predator, or animal that hunts for its food. The hare is prey, or an animal that other animals hunt and eat.

How do predators catch prey? Some predators, such as cheetahs, are faster than their prey and can overtake them. Other predators can keep moving for a long time. For example, wolves can track their prey for hours until the prey wears out. Injecting poison into prey and building a trap to catch prey are other techniques predators use to get their food.

Prey have techniques to avoid being caught. Some prey are fast enough to run, swim, or fly away from their predators. Other prey are poisonous. For example, the sharp spines and deadly skin of porcupine fish make them poisonous if swallowed. Some prey use camouflage. They look enough like their surroundings that the predators don't see them.

The Pharaohs of Ancient Egypt

Around 3000 B.C. a civilization began along the banks of the Nile River in Africa. Today we know this civilization as ancient Egypt.

Pharaohs, or kings, ruled ancient Egypt. The pharaohs were both the religious and military leaders of Egypt. They were the judges and lawmakers, too. Pharaohs owned all the land in Egypt, and had complete power over its people.

Ancient Egyptians believed in life after death. They preserved bodies as mummies and placed the mummies in burial chambers, or tombs. Since pharaohs were so important in life, their tombs were much bigger and more expensive than those of common people. Some of the pharaohs' tombs were great pyramids.

A pharaoh named Tutankhamun had one of the most amazing tombs of all. When archaeologists discovered King Tut's four-room tomb in 1922, they found more than 5,000 objects inside, many covered in gold.

Invisible Planetoids of Mars

"We're on schedule for our Mars landing," astronaut Ari Adams radioed NASA's Mission Control Center.

America's fourth journey to the red planet was going as smoothly as the three previous journeys. Ari and fellow astronauts Louie Wang and Aisha Carter had been training since 2018 to set foot on Mars.

Wham! Their ship banged into something. Louie didn't see anything on the radar. He was wondering what had happened when—*Wham!*—the ship hit something else.

Louie frantically searched the radar. Aisha suited up to check the damage. She found a few deep dents, but nothing critical. As she turned back, her shoulder grazed something. But when she looked around, she saw nothing.

"You know that field of invisible planetoids that no one has been able to find?" asked Aisha when she was back inside. "I think we found it." *Wham! Wham! Wham!* The ship took three more hits in quick succession.

"Let's use the gammapix to find the planetoids and avoid them!" said Ari. Aisha pulled out a bullhorn-shaped device and pointed it out the window. Suddenly, little rainbow-colored, rocklike planetoids were visible. Ari manually steered the ship to Mars without additional hits. The crew had thought nothing could top walking on Mars. But they got a bang out of discovering invisible planetoids, too.

Fireballs of Fury

A saucer hovered over the volcano's crater and then flew inside. Within seconds, the volcano erupted in a river of molten lava. Basketball-sized orbs rose out of the flow and into the air, their energy fueled by whatever—or whoever—had been in the saucer.

Fiery orbs pelted the city nearby. Although it seemed random which buildings, cars, and people were destroyed, the orbs had specific targets. They sought the mean and hurtful and avoided the kind and compassionate.

The attack lasted mere minutes. On the ground, orbs rolled together and transformed into fiery replicas of humans. The city's remaining residents were herded together.

One orb-creature addressed the crowd in a crackly voice. "We will not harm you," it said. "We did what was necessary for the greater good."

People felt devastated by their charred surroundings. They wept for their lost loved ones. *For whose greater good?* they wondered. It was not possible that this had been done for their benefit. They waited.

"We worked hard today to achieve Earth-wide what you see before you," said the orb. "You have a choice: either stay on this scorched planet or come to our planet, where you will work for our greater glory. You must decide now."

What would *you* decide?

Dream Pilot

Aboard the Earth ship *Youngstar*, May 27, 2443

Where do nightmares come from? Some scientists say dreams are what happen when the brain transfers new memories into long-term storage. Others say dreams are just the mind's way of clearing out old junk. But I know the truth. Dreams come from outer space.

I'm a pilot. My job is guiding spacecraft across the vast distances between stars. I'm trained in everything from engine repair to navigation. I can deal with any kind of emergency. But the biggest problem I face during star travel is loneliness.

I am the only one on the ship who stays awake during the long journeys from Earth to other worlds. My fellow explorers sleep through the whole trip, even though it takes months.

This is because starships travel very fast, faster even than the speed of light. The human brain, it turns out, isn't wired to handle that kind of speed. It drives most people crazy. I'm talking the kind of crazy where you foam at the mouth and bark at the moon. And on a long, grueling trip through deep space, you see a lot of moons. So, to avoid going mad, the crew must remain in suspended animation, sleeping the time away. It's a special kind of sleep, not like your nocturnal snooze beneath a comfy blanket. A crew sleeps in special beds that emit electrical signals to block dreams. Because out in space, dreams are very, very bad.

I'm different. When I was a cadet in the Interstellar Exploratory Fleet, doctors determined that with rigorous training my brain would be able to handle the nightmares of deep space. So I became a pilot. A pilot doesn't just fly the ship; he also acts as a fix-it guy and janitor. Also, we never, ever sleep.

"Ready to make the rounds, Chipper?" I ask. Chipper flicks his tail and snuggles up to my legs with a loud meow. He's a special cat in the same way I'm special. He doesn't dream, either, so he keeps me company.

Nearing the halfway point between Earth and the faraway star of Tau Ceti, things are on schedule and going A-OK. I pass through the crew bay where my dozen crewmates recline in their sleep chambers, the machines that keep them safely in slumber humming away. Then, turning down the corridor, I spot a lurking monster. It's an enormous beast, bristling with spiky tufts of fur. It has nothing that looks like a head. Instead, a cluster of serpentine tentacles grows from its neck.

At the end of each tentacle snaps a mouth, ringed in needle-sharp teeth. Shiny, black eyes, like glossy bubbles, blink across its chest. The monster makes a sound like pudding being sucked from a boot.

Chipper and I calmly approach the monster and walk past it. We don't give it a second glance as we leave the corridor. We know it will fade away as long as we pay no attention to it.

One of my daily duties is checking the ship's food banks. The sleeping crew is fed a liquid diet through tubes, and I have to make sure the feeding machines are in good working order. In the galley, I open the cabinet where the food processors are kept.

Inside, a creature with long claws hangs upside down. Its red eyes are the size of grapefruits. Through its translucent skin, I can see branching blood vessels. A little puckered mouth opens wide and out drools hot saliva that sizzles when it touches metal.

I ignore this creature, too, and check the temperature meters on the processors. Unit 3 is running a bit hot, so I adjust the controls and shut the cabinet door.

"Here you go, Chipper," I say, tossing my feline friend a fish-flavored treat before leaving the galley. Chip chews gratefully.

The monsters and bulging eyes and tentacles and teeth are all just my waking nightmares. When ships go faster than the speed of light, space gets twisted and warped around them. And so does the human mind. The brain reacts with hideous thoughts and images—with nightmares. But as awful as they are, I always know they're just dreams.

Or so I think.

I'm about to check on the water recyclers when the ship's alarm bells start screaming. Are we about to collide with an asteroid? Fall into a dark energy cloud? I rush to the cockpit and activate the ship's sensors.

"Something big is out there, Chipper."

A four-engined ship looms in my view screen. The design is nothing like an Earth vessel. How is this possible? Ever since the people of Earth started traveling into space 400-plus years ago, we've never encountered another life-form. But now, right here in front of me, is an alien ship.

Making first contact with aliens is a huge responsibility. According to standard procedure, I must establish communications, determine the nature and intentions of the aliens, and if necessary, defend my ship and crew.

Chipper ducks under my seat, cowering.

Powering up the ship's communication systems, I send a signal to the alien ship.

"Hello. I am the pilot of the Earth ship Youngstar. Please respond."

A terrible noise comes back through the speakers. It's familiar, something I've heard before. It sounds wet and thick, like sucking pudding from a boot.

The ship's computer works to translate the sounds into human language, but the job is too complicated and all I get are garbled sounds.

"Okay, Chipper, I'm going to beam them a visual signal. If there are intelligent life-forms on board, hopefully they'll beam their own visual signal back. Maybe we can figure out a way to communicate with hand signals or something."

Chip makes a pathetic meow.

A moment later, an incoming transmission arrives from the alien ship. I route it to my view screen. And a scream freezes in my throat.

I know this monster. I saw it only several minutes before. It's the creature from the corridor. The one I ignored. The one I believed was only a nightmare. . . .

The tentacles move slowly, like seaweed underwater. The mouths on the ends of its tentacles show their piercing sharp teeth.

It's not alone. In the shadowed spaces behind the creature's control seat hangs another monster, this one with eyes like grapefruit and translucent skin. It's the very same creature I saw in the food processor cabinet.

My nightmares aren't dreams. They're real.

Or else, I've lost my mind to the empty reaches of deep space. I've gone mad!

So I do the only sane thing I can think of. I arm the ship's missiles and place my hand on the launch button . . . .

Aboard the Xraxl ship *Pumrok*, LM-3, XOX79

Where do sleep terrors come from? Our provable data priests have examined this question for many years, and only recently have they learned that dreams originate in telepathic transmissions from intelligent minds. The dream signals travel across the vast distances between stars, and the closer one gets to their originating source, the clearer and more terrifying the dreams become.

I am a pilot, and I am trained to withstand the horrific images that assault me as I guide my ship through the infinite cold dark.

The creature has no head. Instead, tentacles extend from its neck. On the end of each tentacle snaps a mouth with sharp teeth. Dozens of shiny, round eyes bulge from its chest.

Today the images have been very bad. Earlier, when I was maintaining the sulfuric acid tanks with our crew's liquid nourishment, I saw a two-legged, two-armed creature. A strange, bulging oval-shaped thing grew from its neck, topped by a tuft of fur, with two eyes peering out. At its feet was a small furred creature with a mobile tail and twitching whiskers. It made a bizarre purring noise.

I ignored them, of course, understanding they were nothing but distant telepathic transmissions from very far away. But now, hovering before my ship, is an alien vessel. Its pilot appears in my visual monitors. It is the creature from my waking sleep terrors!

Hanging behind me, Gafl, my pet jigbite, drools nervously, her saliva sizzling on the ship's deck plates.

"Greetings, alien," I say. "My name is Pilot Gud-Zon, from the Xraxl ship *Pumrok*. I greet you in peace."

The hinged flesh flap in the lower quadrant of the bulge growing from the strange creature's neck moves up and down. The horrifying creature says something that sounds like, "*Rarrblah mmurgh blah*." It is completely untranslatable by my ship's computer.

But a moment later, my sensors make one thing completely clear: The alien has armed its weapons systems and is preparing to fire. I have no choice but to activate my proton cannons and reduce the alien ship to smithereens. Unless . . .

What if I can somehow convince the creature that I mean it no harm? That my people are peaceful travelers? That my intentions are gentle?

I can think of only one thing.

"Come here, Gafl," I say, pulling down my jigbite from her perch. "Sit with me."

My locomotion tentacles are her favorite place to sit, and as I pet her spikes, she drools acid in delight.

On my view screen, the alien's hideous face remains unreadable. But it moves its five-pronged appendage away from its weapons controls.

Then it turns to the yowling little creature at its feet. "*Bargle blahman blurt,*" it says, and it places the little creature on its lap. The little creature makes its purring sound, which I now realize is a contented sound.

In that moment, I know we will not fall to each other's weapons systems. Because we have both demonstrated a similar quality. The alien may be a horrendous, awful, fearsome creature—like something out of sleep terrors—but in the end, it is just like me.

It is a person.

I smile at it with all of my mouths. The hinged flesh flap in the lower part of the oval bulge turns upward. I believe that the alien, though hideous still, is smiling back at me.

Reread the Story

Analyze the Characters, Setting, and Plot

- Who are the characters in the story?
- Where and when does the story take place?
- What is peculiar about the first pilot's job?
- What is the main problem in this story?
- How is the problem resolved?
- What unusual event happens at the end of the story?

Focus on Comprehension: Summarize Information

- Write a one-sentence summary describing the first pilot's job.
- What events should be included in a summary of the first pilot's rounds?
- In one sentence, summarize the end of the science fiction story.

Analyze the Tools Writers Use: Strong Lead

- Reread the lead for this science fiction story. What type of lead did the author use? How can you tell?
- Did the lead hook you as a reader? Why?
- In what other ways could this lead have been written?

Focus on Unnamed Main Characters

All stories have characters, and more often than not, these characters have names. Every now and then, authors choose not to name their main characters. The pilot in the first ship is not named. How does this affect the story?

Focus on Words: Word Origins

Make a chart like the one below. Locate each word in the book. Use a dictionary or the Internet to identify the word's origin and its history, such as when it was first used and by whom. Finally, write a definition for the word. One example is provided.

Page	Word	Word Origin	Word History	Definition
55	nocturnal	nocturnus	Middle French/Latin; fifteenth century	occurring at night
56	recline			
56	serpentine			
56	translucent			
57	pathetic			
59	mobile			
60	appendage			

A Fun Debate

Moderator: This is a debate between Selma Crump, Director of Fun, and Frank Rombo, Vice President of Finance, at the LaughOutLoud Amusement Park! Tonight they will debate building a new fun house at the park.

Selma: I think a fun house is essential to any amusement park. Did you know that last year alone, 3,457 people e-mailed us asking for a fun house?

Frank: Why do we need a fun house? Nobody likes fun houses anymore.

Selma: You have no sense of fun!

Frank: That's not true! Last year I received the "Best Sense of Humor" award from the National Fun Club! Only eight people have ever received that award. But getting back to the issue: The park doesn't have enough money to build a fun house.

Selma: That's not true! Ms. Lily Hogan has written us a check for the amount a fun house would cost to build.

Frank: I have a petition here signed by thirteen neighbors who don't want a fun house.

Selma: And I have a petition signed by 1,465 people who do!

Moderator: That's all we have time for. We'll announce the winner of the debate in a few minutes.

Wild Weather (Excerpt 1)

Narrator: Jen downloads "Wild Weather," which begins innocently enough. They learn that each player will be asked a question about the weather. A correct answer will allow that player to choose any place on Earth and create weather for it. A computer simulation instantly shows what happens.

Jen: I'm first. My question is, "What happens when water droplets in the cold upper regions of a thundercloud keep colliding into one another until layers of ice form around them?" That's easy: you get hailstones. Now we get to click on any part of the world and create instant weather for it.

Max: I've always wondered what it would look like if it snowed in the tropics.

Jen: Okay, I'm picking a small island in the South Pacific that doesn't have any people on it.

Max: What does that matter?

Jen: It's not right to make unsuspecting people freeze to death, even if they are computer-generated, Max! Okay, now I'll click on "blizzard" and hit enter.

Max: Look at that! Palm trees covered with snow! It's fun to control the weather. Hey wait, isn't that an airplane in the sky over the island? Why would an airplane be in a computer simulation?

Dad: Kids, come in here immediately! Something amazing is happening!

Narrator: Jen and Max run into the living room. A special weather bulletin is on TV.

Mom: This is incredible. How could it be happening?

Sonny: No, you're not dreaming, folks—that's snow falling on a tiny tropical island in the Pacific. We're getting this video live from our "What's Up with the Weather?" plane checking on the tropical storm we told you about earlier.

Heather: This is no tropical storm, Sonny. At the rate this snow is falling, I'd say it's a good old-fashioned blizzard!

Mom and Dad: Oh, my!

Jen and Max: Uh-oh!

Wild Weather (Excerpt 2)

Narrator: Something strange is about to happen at the McCloud home. Middle-school students Jen and Max are going to find out just how dangerous it can be to mess with Mother Nature. But for the moment, all is calm. So let's join Mr. and Mrs. McCloud, Jen, and Max as they prepare to watch their favorite TV show.

Dad: I have a feeling that "What's Up with the Weather?" is going to be exciting tonight. I'm getting that tingly feeling I get when it is about to rain, only more intense.

Mom: Hurry, Max and Jen! The show's about to start.

Jen: I was just putting the finishing touches on my report on extreme weather.

Max: And I was finishing a chapter in this cool new book about—

Dad: Do that after the show. Shh! The theme music is over, which means—

Sonny: Good evening, weather watchers. This is Sonny Skye, your Weather Guy.

Heather: And I'm Heather Shady, your Weather Lady.

Mom, Dad, Jen, and Max: Hi, Sonny! Hi, Heather!

Sonny: Welcome to another edition of "What's Up with the Weather?"—the show that reports on newsworthy weather all over the world.

Heather: We've got a captivating show this evening. We'll have live footage of a tropical storm forming in the Pacific Ocean that may develop into a full-scale hurricane.

Mom: That means winds blowing at over seventy-five miles per hour.

Sonny: But first, we want to alert our viewers in the northern states that a large storm on the sun has created some strong solar winds. These can cause an *aurora borealis*, also called the Northern Lights. The Northern Lights can provide a spectacular display of shimmering light in the sky.

Mom, Dad, Jen, and Max: We already know that!

Heather: We're expecting the display to begin around midnight tomorrow. Clear skies are predicted, so be sure to set up chairs in your backyard and enjoy the show!

Unit 5

Table of Contents

Mars and Earth

Of all the known planets in our solar system, Mars is most similar to Earth. Like Earth, Mars has clouds, fog, canyons, and mountains. The north and south poles on Mars are covered with ice, just like Earth's poles. Earth and Mars both have seasons, too.

There are also differences between Mars and Earth. Earth's diameter, or distance across, is about 7,926 miles (12,756 kilometers). In contrast, the diameter of Mars is only about 4,222 miles (6,795 kilometers.)

Another difference between Mars and Earth is color. Mars looks reddish from space because of the iron in its soil. Earth, on the other hand, looks blue, due to the oceans that cover most of its surface.

Mars and Earth both have mountains, but there are big differences in the mountains' heights. The tallest mountain on Mars, Olympus Mons, is 16 miles (25.7 kilometers) high. Mount Everest, the tallest mountain on Earth, is just 5.4 miles (8.6 kilometers) high.

Immigration in the 1840s

The United States has always been a nation of immigrants, or people who move to the country from other countries. In the early 1840s, most of the immigrants were from Ireland and Germany.

Most Irish people went to the United States because they were poor and hungry. German immigrants, on the other hand, had money. Unlike the Irish, who were mostly farmers, many German immigrants were shopkeepers and crafts workers.

Like the Irish, most German immigrants settled in northeastern United States. Immigrants from both countries often settled in cities.

German immigrants were likely to open stores or work in crafts positions such as carpentry. Many Irish, by contrast, worked in factories and in construction.

Athens and Sparta

Athens and Sparta were two of the most powerful city-states in ancient Greece. Each city-state was more like a country than a city. Both city-states ruled the land all around them.

Athens and Sparta had many similarities. Both had agoras, or open-air market places. Both had gymnasiums, where boys received physical and military training.

But Athens and Sparta were different in many ways, too. In Athens, young men trained to be soldiers, while also learning to give public speeches and play musical instruments. In Sparta, however, the greatest honor for a young man was to die defending his city-state.

Women in Athens and in Sparta had very different lives. In Athens, most young women did not go to school. They did not engage in business or participate in sports. In Sparta, on the other hand, girls could participate in athletic activities and get an education. Many Spartan women were active in business.

Athens, Greece

Thor's Magic Hammer

Long ago, Thor, the Norse god of thunder, was shocked to discover that his magic hammer was missing. Without it, he couldn't create thunder and lightning. Thor asked Loki, a shape-shifting god, for help. Loki turned into a falcon and flew off to look for Thor's hammer. He learned that the king of the giants had stolen it. The king would return it if he could marry Freya, the goddess of love.

When Loki presented the giant's terms, Freya refused to marry a hideous giant. The gods held a meeting to figure out what to do. They decided to trick the giant in order to retrieve Thor's hammer. They said Thor should pretend to be Freya. Thor reluctantly dressed in bridal clothes and a veil, Loki disguised himself as a maidservant, and the two set off.

At a pre-wedding feast, the king of the giants was amazed at the appetite of his bride-to-be. When he lifted the veil, he saw Thor's eyes glowering angrily at him. Loki told him the bride had not slept in anticipation of the wedding.

The giant believed Loki and called for the magic hammer to be brought to bless his bride. At the sight of it, Thor ripped off his disguise, grabbed the hammer, and killed the giant king with it.

Thor killed every giant in the banquet hall, too. Then Thor and Loki went home. To celebrate the return of his hammer, Thor created the fiercest thunder and lightning storm the world had ever seen.

Narcissus

Back in the time of the Greek gods, Narcissus was the handsomest man in Greece. Many women admired him and vied for his attention. Nymphs, the young maiden spirits of nature, longed for him too. Narcissus knew how handsome he was and what effect he had on people. His personality, however, did not match his looks. He thought very highly of himself and did not care about others. He rejected every admirer, not bothering to be kind about it.

Narcissus broke many hearts. One rejected nymph prayed that he too would feel unrequited love. The goddess Nemesis heard and answered her prayer.

While hunting one day, Narcissus leaned over a pool of water to get a drink. For the first time he saw his own reflection but, thanks to Nemesis, he did not know he was looking at himself. He fell instantly in love with the image he saw. He reached out to touch it, but it remained beyond his grasp.

Eventually Narcissus realized he was looking at himself. "Now I know how others have felt!" he cried. "I know what it feels like to pine for a love you cannot have." Narcissus stared and stared at his reflection, never moving from the pool. He eventually died there, and a handsome flower we know as the narcissus grew in his place.

QUETZALCOATL CREATES PEOPLE

AN AZTEC MYTH

Long ago, there were people on Earth. But some of the gods were displeased with the way the people were living their lives. They created a great flood that destroyed all the people. After all that destruction, the other gods looked down at Earth and discussed what they saw.

"Earth is still a lush sea of beauty," said the goddess Milky Way.

"If only there could be people populating this splendid place once again," said Star Goddess wistfully.

Milky Way and Star Goddess remained silent for a time. Then, as though they were sharing the same thought, they turned in unison to look at Quetzalcoatl, the feathered serpent god.

"Quetzalcoatl," said Star Goddess, "only you are clever enough and brave enough to create viable new life."

"We are sure that under your caring guidance, the people you create will be well-bred and responsible," said Milky Way.

Quetzalcoatl considered what the gods were getting at and said, "You are asking me to perform a great feat, one fraught with danger."

This modern painting of Quetzalcoatl hangs in a museum in Mexico City, Mexico.

"Yes, we are," said Star Goddess. "You must go to the Land of the Dead and collect the bones of those who died long ago."

"It is difficult and risky, we know," said Milky Way. "Yum Cimil, the death god, is full of malice. There is a chance you will not make it back. But we know you can do it."

Quetzalcoatl accepted the task and headed down under the surface of Earth toward Yum Cimil and his dreaded Land of the Dead.

"Who goes there?" bellowed a loud and ominous voice. It belonged to the god Yum Cimil, a volatile malcontent. He could be a volcano of anger.

"It is I, Quetzalcoatl. I have come for the bones of the dead."

"My bones?" scoffed the death god. "You cannot take my prized possessions!"

"The bones are not yours, Yum Cimil," said Quetzalcoatl tersely. "They are the bones of the Earth's ancestors. We will use them to create new humans to populate the planet."

"And what makes you think they will fare better than the last batch of wretched beings?" asked the lord of the dead menacingly as he stroked his pet owl.

"They will flourish with the proper guidance," said Quetzalcoatl. "And I will give it to them."

Yum Cimil thought for a moment. He had no intention of giving the bones to Quetzalcoatl. But because he was a maladjusted and malevolent god, he decided to play a trick on the good god.

"You may have the bones, Quetzalcoatl, but first you must blow this conch shell to announce our arrangement. The louder the sound, the more bones you can take. But if you make no sound, then you must stay with me for eternity."

That did not seem like an unrealistic request or difficult task for Quetzalcoatl. He took the conch shell and blew with all his might. But there was no sound! He tried again, inhaling so deeply that the trees bent. Then he released a tornado from his lungs. Still there was no sound.

Quetzalcoatl turned the shell around in his hands and quickly realized the shell was a sound trap. "There is a hole to blow into, but no other holes in the shell, so no sound can get out."

"No sound, no bones!" said Yum Cimil with a sinister laugh.

"I see that the lord of the dead is playing one of his tricks on me. Well, I have some tricks, too."

Quetzalcoatl summoned the worms that dwelled in the Land of the Dead to come forward. Then he commanded them to burrow holes in the conch. Next Quetzalcoatl called forth all of the hornets that dwelled in the Land of the Dead. The hornets flew into the conch and buzzed ferociously. Finally, Quetzalcoatl put the conch to his lips once more and blew as hard as he could again.

The shrill whistling sound blasting from the shell coupled with the buzzing of the hornets rattled the lord of the dead.

"He is a powerful foe!" exclaimed Yum Cimil, clasping his ears.

"The bones," said Quetzalcoatl as he strode toward the lord of the dead, hands outstretched.

"Bah! Take them," said the lord of the dead.

Quetzalcoatl gathered up the bones of the people of the past world and then made his way up the tunnel that led to the surface of Earth.

But the lord of the dead wasn't about to give up that easily. He created a large chasm. Quetzalcoatl fell into it, down, down, down, crashing against sharp rocks and breaking all of the bones he was carrying.

Quetzalcoatl's hopes for a new, improved breed of people were dashed as he looked down at the fragments of bones in his arms. They were splinters of kindling in his dwelling. Disappointed but undaunted, he righted himself and made his way back to the surface.

Quetzalcoatl headed toward the dwelling of Serpent Woman, for she owned the sacred pestle with which to grind the bones into a powder. Quetzalcoatl had an idea about how to turn the pieces of bones into humans yet.

Serpent Woman agreed to help Quetzalcoatl but explained, "There is one problem. These humans will be different sizes. Those made from the large pieces of bone will be large and those made from the smaller pieces will be small."

terra-cotta sculpture of the Aztec god of death

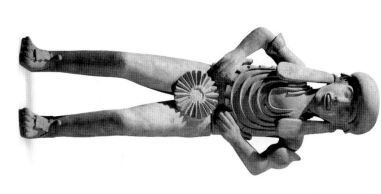

73

Quetzalcoatl nodded his head thoughtfully. "That will be fine, even better. For the world should be populated with all kinds of people.

Serpent Woman placed the powder in a golden bowl and handed it to Quetzalcoatl. He added a drop of his blood and stirred, explaining, "By adding a drop of my blood to the powder, I am giving life to the old bones."

From this mixture were formed new people. Some were tall and some were small. Some were sturdy and others were more delicate. But all were beautiful in the eyes of Quetzalcoatl, who nearly sacrificed himself to give them life.

This painting of Quetzalcoatl dates back to the 1500s.

REREAD THE MYTH

Analyze the Characters, Setting, and Plot

- Who are the main characters in the myth?
- Who are the minor characters in the myth?
- What is the problem in this myth?
- On what mission is Quetzalcoatl sent?
- How does Yum Cimil react when Quetzalcoatl asks him for the bones?
- What trick does Yum Cimil play on Quetzalcoatl?
- What happens to Quetzalcoatl after he receives the bones?
- How does the myth end?

Focus on Comprehension: Summarize Information

- Write a two- to three-sentence summary for the beginning of this myth.
- What information should be included in a summary of how Quetzalcoatl outsmarted Yum Cimil?
- In one sentence, summarize the end of the myth.

Analyze the Tools Writers Use: Metaphor

- On page 71, the goddess Milky Way says, "Earth is still a lush sea of beauty." Explain how this is a metaphor.
- On page 72, the author says that Yum Cimil could be a volcano of anger. What does the author mean?

- On page 72, the author says that Quetzalcoatl released a tornado from his lungs. What two things are being compared?
- On page 73, the author says that the bones Quetzalcoatl held were splinters of kindling in his hands. Explain how this is a metaphor.

Focus on Words: Prefixes (mal)

Mal is another example of prefixes more advanced writers use. **Mal** means "bad" as in **malformed** and **malaise**. Make a chart like the one below. Read each word in the chart. For each word, identify its part of speech as it is used in the myth. Then explain how the prefix changes the meaning of the base or root word.

Page	Word	Part of Speech	How Prefix Changes Meaning of Base or Root Word
72	malice		
72	malcontent		
72	maladjusted		
72	malevolent		

Mystery Solved

Kyra finished washing the dishes and reached for her ring on the windowsill. It was gone! Frantically, she searched all around the sink and on the floor. Then she combed through the bushes outside under the open window. "No ring, and no footprints, either," Kyra mused thoughtfully.

Kyra decided to try to catch the thief in the act. She took off one of her gold earrings and put it on the windowsill. She crawled into the broom closet, leaving the door open just a crack so she could see the earring. Then she waited . . . and waited.

Kyra stared at the earring shining in the sunlight until she almost fell asleep. She jerked awake, upsetting the many objects in the crowded closet. CRASH! BANG! "Ow!" yelped Kyra. It took her a long time to free herself and put the closet in order again. "Well, that didn't go well," she sighed.

Then Kyra noticed it: The earring was gone! She rushed outside again. Still there were no footprints. She looked up at one of the trees and saw an old red ribbon of hers hanging from a bird's nest.

Quickly, Kyra got a ladder from the garage and climbed up to the nest. In it she found a piece of broken glass, some foil, and both her ring and her earring! The thief was a crow.

Odyssey (Excerpt 1)

Narrator 1: Odysseus was a legendary Greek ruler whose quick thinking helped win the Trojan War around 1200 B.C. After the war, he set sail from the ancient city of Troy for his home on Ithaca, an island off the west coast of Greece.

Odysseus: I will return you safely to your families.

Eurylochus: All twelve ships are in the harbor and ready to sail, my lord.

Narrator 2: Along the way Odysseus and his men had many adventures. Their first was at the land of the Cyclops, the one-eyed giant.

Odysseus: Let us see who lives on this island. We shall take twelve men and a jar of the wine that Apollo's priest gave us.

Narrator 1: The men walked until they reached a giant cave surrounded by dozens of sheep.

Eurylochus: I wonder where the shepherd is.

Odysseus: Let's go inside the cave and look around.

Elpeenor: These wheels of cheese are as tall as I am! And I could bathe in these buckets of milk!

Castor: Great Zeus! The earth is shaking and a shadow is darkening the mouth of the cave! Look, it is a giant, an ugly, one-eyed giant, and he looks mean!

Polyphemus: (*roaring*) Who trespasses in my home?

Odysseus: We are Greek warriors. We have stopped here on our long journey home.

Polyphemus: Silence! Do you not know that I am the terrible Cyclops, Polyphemus, son of Poseidon, god of the sea?

Odysseus: Then where is your hospitality, Polyphemus? We are your guests.

Polyphemus: Hospitality? Do you expect me to have you to dinner? Ha! I will have you for dinner . . . and for breakfast and lunch, as well.

Narrator 2: The Cyclops grabbed two of the men and quickly gobbled them. The others froze in fear. Then Cyclops brought his sheep inside the cave and blocked the entrance with a giant boulder.

Odyssey (Excerpt 2)

Odysseus: We must be careful. This is a strange place, and we have lost many men already. Eurylochus, take half our men and see who lives in that white castle in the distance, then report back to me.

Narrator 1: The men walked until they came to the castle, which was surrounded by wild animals.

Castor: Lions and tigers surround the castle! They're sure to eat us. I refuse to go any closer!

Narrator 2: Just then, a beautiful woman walked out of the castle. In one hand she carried a slender wooden stick. In another, she carried a tray laden with bread, wine, and cheese.

Circe: Do not be afraid, travelers. I am Circe and these, um, these animals, are my pets. They are completely harmless.

Elpeenor: They are as tame as my dog in Ithaca; why, look at how they wag their tails!

Circe: Sit. You look tired and hungry. Eat!

Eurylochus: Wait. I'm not sure if I trust her. There's something about the way she clutches that stick, and those animals . . . It's unnatural. They are so tame they appear almost . . . human.

Elpeenor: Go back to the ship if you want to, Eurylochus, but we're staying.

Eurylochus: (*quietly*) I'll just keep an eye on things from behind this tree.

Elpeenor: This food is delicious, Circe. I hope you've got lots more.

Castor: Yes, I hope you've got lots more because we're so hungry! Gobble, gobble, gobble.

Circe: Fools! Since you behave like pigs, pigs you shall become! *Meta! Meta! Meta!* Now you are swine!

Elpeenor and Castor: Snort, snort.

Eurylochus: I knew that was more than a stick—it's a magic wand. And she's used it to turn our men into pigs! I must tell Odysseus.

Narrator 1: Eurylochus ran to find Odysseus.

Eurylochus: An enchantress named Circe lives on this island, and she has turned our men into pigs!

Odysseus: What?! I will find that enchantress and make her turn my charges back into men! Let's go.

Unit 6

Table of Contents

Hercules

According to Greek myth, Hercules was half-god and half-human. The King of Mycenae owned Hercules. The king told Hercules that if he wanted to be free, he must perform twelve difficult and dangerous physical tasks, or labors.

Hercules performed ten of the tasks, which included slaying a lion and taming man-eating horses. He was exhausted as he said to the king, "Because I have completed these ten terrible labors, surely, I have earned my freedom now!"

"No," responded the king, "they are not enough. For your eleventh labor, you must capture some of the golden apples that belong to the goddess Hera and bring them to me."

Hercules knew that the Hesperides, daughters of a giant named Atlas, guarded the golden apples. A fierce dragon with many heads also guarded them. Hercules was able to shoot straight and strong with his bow and arrow; therefore, he could slay the dragon. But how would he get past the Hesperides?

Pike's Peak or Bust!

In 1858, some men struck gold near Pike's Peak in the Rocky Mountains. As a result, thousands of wagons filled with gold seekers were soon rolling across the Great Plains toward the Rocky Mountains. Because these gold seekers, or prospectors, were headed for Pike's Peak, they often had "Pike's Peak or Bust" painted on the sides of their wagons.

As soon as the prospectors reached the foothills of the Rockies, they set up tents and shacks, resulting in mining camps all around the area. The prospectors needed services and supplies. Consequently, general stores, hotels, and blacksmith shops sprang up in the mining camps. Mining camps quickly became mining towns.

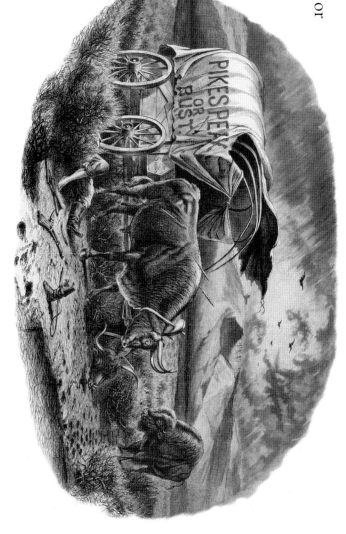

Some of these mining towns disappeared when the gold nearby ran out. But other mining towns grew and prospered. One of these mining towns became Denver, the capital of Colorado.

The *Challenger* Disaster

On January 28, 1986, at 11:38 A.M., the space shuttle *Challenger* blasted off from its launch pad at the Kennedy Space Center in Florida. The excitement of the successful takeoff soon turned to horror as the *Challenger* exploded and burst into flames as the world watched. All seven people aboard died, including Christa McAuliffe, the first teacher in space.

The *Challenger* had previously flown nine successful missions. What caused the tenth mission to end in such a dreadful tragedy?

Investigators soon discovered what caused the tragedy—two small parts of the shuttle, the O-rings, malfunctioned. The O-rings were supposed to seal in the hot gases created during ignition. Cold temperatures the morning of liftoff caused the O-rings to fail. As a result, the super hot gases leaked out. These gases ignited the fuel tank, which led to the explosion of the *Challenger*.

Rachel Carson

Rachel Carson led the fight to control pollution. She was a scientist and author who loved nature. She urged people to take better care of the planet.

Rachel was born on a farm in Pennsylvania in 1907. From the time she was a little girl, Rachel loved animals and all nature.

When she grew up, Rachel became a marine biologist. She got a job with the U.S. Fish and Wildlife Service, where she wrote about the natural world. She also wrote for magazines and newspapers. Many of her articles were about the effects of pollution on rivers and oceans.

Pesticides were one kind of pollution that concerned Rachel. Pesticides were sprayed to kill insects. Rachel knew, though, that they could harm people, other animals, and plants, too. Rachel said pesticides must "not destroy us along with insects."

Her most famous book, *Silent Spring*, was the first book that called for pesticide control. *Silent Spring* paved the way for policies that would protect people and the planet, not only from pesticides but also from pollutants such as lead, mercury, and carbon monoxide. It was first published in 1962, but it is still read today.

Rachel died in 1964. In 1980, she was honored with the Presidential Medal of Freedom for her important work.

Mary Leakey

Mary Leakey was an important archaeologist. She worked on digs, studying ancient materials. Leakey learned a lot about early humans.

Mary Leakey was born in London, England, in 1913. When she was a child, she and her parents visited places where archaeologists were hard at work. Leakey loved what she saw. She knew what she wanted to do when she grew up.

As an adult, Mary Leakey worked with her husband, Louis. They went on digs in Africa. Their work there led to many important discoveries.

In 1948, Mary Leakey found a very important skull. It belonged to someone who was probably related to both apes and humans. It was the first skull like that ever found. The skull was 18 million years old!

In 1978, Leakey discovered footprints of someone who walked upright. Humans walk upright. Apes do not. The footprints were 3.5 million years old. They were the oldest ones like that!

Mary Leakey died in 1996. Thanks to the work that she and her husband did, scientists now believe that human life began in Africa.

Cleopatra

What is it about Cleopatra, the last queen of Egypt, that has fascinated writers and artists for centuries?

It's difficult to confirm the facts of Cleopatra's life. So much about her is unknown or has been slanted by later writers. After her death, the Romans intentionally destroyed many of the documents of her reign. Later accounts of Cleopatra's life were written by Greek and Roman writers, who either vilified her as an evil temptress, or embellished descriptions of her beauty, talents, and accomplishments. The lines blur between fact and myth.

What is certain is that Cleopatra was highly intelligent and courageous, a wise administrator, and fiercely loyal to the two men she loved, one for whom she sacrificed her life.

The Struggle for the Throne

Cleopatra was born in Alexandria, Egypt, in 69 B.C.E. Not much is known about her early years. Many people are surprised to learn that she was Greek, a descendant of the Macedonian general Ptolemy. She may have had light-colored hair and, judging from her images on coins and statues, was certainly striking in appearance.

This oil painting from 1637 is called Caesar Leads Cleopatra Back to the Throne of Egypt.

Cleopatra spoke many languages, including Greek, Egyptian, and Syrian. The fact that she spoke Egyptian, the language of her subjects, set her apart from the other Ptolemies, none of whom deigned to learn the language of the people over whom they ruled.

When Cleopatra was 18, her father, Ptolemy XI, died, leaving her and her 10-year-old brother to rule together. They were supposed to marry one another, according to Egyptian custom. But they did not get along. Young Ptolemy XIII's advisers drove Cleopatra out of Egypt and probably planned to have her killed.

Meanwhile, one of the Roman triumvirs, Pompey, was murdered in Egypt in 48 B.C.E. Four days later, Julius Caesar arrived in Egypt. Caesar learned from his barber that Cleopatra's brother and his advisers were planning to kill him. So he sent for Cleopatra, probably with the intention of forming an alliance with her. In a characteristically bold move, Cleopatra had herself rolled into a carpet and was brought to Caesar's room in secret. She was 21. Caesar was 52.

Did they fall in love immediately? No one knows for certain. Her intelligence and beauty seem to have charmed Caesar. What did she see in this much-older man? Cleopatra was a practical person. She needed help opposing her brother, and it was handy to partner with the most powerful man in the Western world. Still, it seems evident that their admiration quickly became mutual.

Caesar promptly backed Cleopatra against her brother. He had Ptolemy's advisers assassinated. Then he sent for reinforcements, and the Roman army vanquished the Egyptians who had been plotting to kill Caesar. Ptolemy was drowned as he tried to flee from the Roman troops.

Cleopatra married her surviving brother, 12-year-old Ptolemy XIV, and ascended the throne. She was now the reigning queen of Egypt.

Life After Caesar

Caesar returned to Rome in 47 B.C.E., bringing with him Cleopatra and their young son, Caesarion, as his official guests. Many Romans were appalled that the Egyptian queen had come to Rome to be near the married Caesar.

A few years later, after Caesar was murdered, Cleopatra fled back to Egypt.

About a year after Caesar's death, three powerful Romans formed a second triumvirate. One was Caesar's 18-year-old adopted son, his grandnephew Octavian. (Caesar had left no legitimate male heirs.) The second was a general named Marcus Lepidus. The third was one of Caesar's most trusted military generals, a man named Marcus Antonius (or Mark Antony, or just Antony). Meanwhile, Caesar's two main assassins, Brutus and Cassius, began raising troops in Greece to fight the new triumvirs.

By now Egypt's treasury had recovered from the misrule of Cleopatra's father. Thanks to Cleopatra's expansion of agriculture and sound administrative decisions regarding exports to other countries of grain, linen, and oil, Egypt had grown wealthy again.

Cleopatra was forced to choose sides in the Roman conflict. Should she support the power-hungry triumvirs or the men who had murdered Caesar? Cleopatra, fiercely loyal to her dead lover, sided with the triumvirs. In 42 B.C.E., Brutus and Cassius went to war against Antony and Octavian in northern Greece. Brutus and Cassius were defeated, and both committed suicide. Thus ended the Roman Republic.

Mark Antony

Cleopatra, Antony, and Octavian

The three triumvirs divided the Roman empire among themselves, assigning each a portion over which to rule.

Antony was granted power over Greece, Asia Minor, and Cleopatra's Egypt. He hoped to conquer Parthia for Rome, but knew he needed vast sums of money to wage the campaign—and Cleopatra was rich. So in the summer of 41 B.C.E., he summoned Cleopatra, who was now about 28 years old, to his headquarters in Tarsus (in southern Asia Minor).

According to a Greek writer and historian named Plutarch, Cleopatra made a memorable entrance. She sailed up the river in a barge with a golden stern and heavily perfumed purple sails. Her rowers, beautiful handmaidens to the queen, dipped their silver oars in time to the music of a flute. People came running from all directions to watch.

Whether or not this story is true, Cleopatra had proven to be a master at creating a dramatic public image of herself. She shrewdly relied on visual spectacle, as few of the people in her kingdom knew how to read and write. Antony appears to have been instantly smitten with her.

This fresco painting of Antony and Cleopatra is by Giovanni Tiepolo, a famous Italian artist of the 1700s.

The queen made an agreement with Antony. In exchange for his protection against her enemies, she promised to provide him with money to fund his military campaign.

Whatever her initial motives for forming an alliance with Antony, Cleopatra soon fell in love with him. Forgetting that he had an empire to rule, Antony remained in Alexandria with Cleopatra over the winter. She became pregnant with his child.

In 40 B.C.E., Antony left Cleopatra to travel back to Rome. While he had been gone, his wife, Fulvia, and brother, Lucius, had led a failed rebellion against Octavian.

Antony repaired his relations with Octavian. Soon after that, Fulvia died. Antony married Octavian's sister, Octavia, in order to cement the bond between the two triumvirs. A few weeks after Antony's marriage, Cleopatra gave birth to twins—Antony was the father. With Antony in Rome, the ever-practical Cleopatra spent the next several years concentrating on ruling her kingdom and increasing the Egyptian treasury. In so doing, she became one of the richest and most powerful women in the world.

In 37 B.C.E., Antony left for Syria, intent on waging war against Parthia. He soon sent for Cleopatra. His campaign against the Parthians failed, but he remained with Cleopatra, leaving his sad wife, Octavia, back in Rome.

In 35 B.C.E., Cleopatra gave birth to her third child by Antony. Antony established Cleopatra and her son Caesarion as joint rulers of Egypt and Cyprus. He also bestowed titles and lands in the eastern provinces on the children he had fathered with Cleopatra. Many Romans were shocked by his behavior.

Back in Rome, Octavian removed Lepidus from power and had him arrested. Octavian then set about stirring up Roman anger against Antony. Octavian denounced Antony's abandonment of Octavia. He convinced the Senate that Cleopatra had bewitched Antony and was scheming to take over the empire.

In 32 B.C.E., the shrewd Octavian declared war—not against the popular Antony, but against Cleopatra. Privately, he knew that by waging war against Antony, he was waging war against Antony. If Octavian defeated Antony, he would become the sole ruler of the new Roman Empire.

Last Days Together

Antony and Cleopatra raised a huge army to fight Octavian. They recruited soldiers from the eastern provinces, many of whom hoped to gain independence from Rome.

In 30 B.C.E., an immense battle took place at Actium, in western Greece. Octavian's troops prevailed. Antony and Cleopatra fled to Alexandria. They knew that all was now lost.

Octavian sent a message to Cleopatra. He told her that if she agreed to kill Antony, her own life would be spared. Octavian underestimated Cleopatra's love and loyalty. She refused.

Meanwhile, Antony received a message that Cleopatra was dead. Having lost the battle with Octavian, and believing his beloved to be dead, he must have despaired of having anything more to live for. According to Plutarch's version of the story, Antony stabbed himself with his sword. Servants carried the mortally wounded man to Cleopatra. He died in her arms.

Tragic End

Cleopatra was now 39 years old, and though still living in her palace, she was a virtual prisoner of Octavian. Octavian, who clearly respected her, seemed to have no intention of executing her. But she was convinced she would be taken to Rome and paraded before the people as a conquered queen. To spare herself such humiliation, she dressed herself in royal robes and poisoned herself with the bite of a deadly asp, a type of snake. Her handmaidens did the same.

Octavian honored Cleopatra's wish to be buried next to Antony. But to avoid any future power struggles, he ordered the child she had borne with Caesar, Caesarion, to be slain.

In a purely noble act, Antony's sad and neglected wife, Octavia, took in Antony and Cleopatra's children and raised them as her own.

Octavian became known as Augustus Caesar, the first leader of the Roman Empire. Egypt's long history as an independent nation came to an end.

But Cleopatra's story—her incredible life, her capacity for love and loyalty, her tragic death, and her unparalleled mystique—lives on to this day.

This 1769 oil painting shows Octavian at Cleopatra's deathbed.

Reread the Biography

Analyze the Subject

- When and where was Cleopatra born?
- What were some of Cleopatra's accomplishments?
- What kind of challenges did Cleopatra face?
- Many people were involved in Cleopatra's life. Identify three and explain their involvement in her life.
- Under what conditions did Cleopatra's life end?
- Would you want to have Cleopatra's power? Why or why not?

Focus on Comprehension: Identify Main Idea and Supporting Details

- "Life After Caesar" is about some of the things Cleopatra did after Caesar was murdered. What details support this main idea?
- Identify two stated main ideas in this biography.
- The last section is about Cleopatra's last days. What details support this main idea?

Focus on Including Questions

Many authors include questions in biographies because they make readers stop and think while they are reading. Identify places in the text where the author included questions. What do those questions make you think about? How do they help you understand the biography?

Analyze the Tools Writers Use: Strong Lead

- Reread the lead for this biography. What type of lead did the author use? Direct or indirect? How can you tell?
- Did the lead "hook" you as a reader? Why?
- What did you expect to learn after reading the lead?
- In what other ways could this lead have been written?

Focus on Words: Word Origins

Make a chart like the one below. Use a dictionary or the Internet to identify each word's origin and its history, such as when it was first used and by whom. Finally, write a definition for the word.

Page	Word	Word Origins	Word History	Definition
85	administrator			
87	agriculture			
88	spectacle			
90	mortally			

© 2014 Benchmark Education Company, LLC

The Wind

by Robert Louis Stevenson

I saw you toss the kites on high
And blow the birds about the sky;
And all around I heard you pass,
Like ladies' skirts across the grass—
  O wind, a-blowing all day long,
  O wind, that sings so loud a song!

I saw the different things you did,
But always you yourself you hid.
I felt you push, I heard you call,
I could not see yourself at all—
  O wind, a-blowing all day long,
  O wind, that sings so loud a song!

O you that are so strong and cold,
O blower, are you young or old?
Are you a beast of field and tree
Or just a stronger child than me?
  O wind, a-blowing all day long,
  O wind, that sings so loud a song!

Clara Barton: Angel of the Battlefield
(Excerpt 1)

Dad: Tammy, I'm so glad you and Tommy have vacation this week. Your mother and I both have to finish writing our books. You can help me with my research.

Tammy: I always like to go on *When Machine* trips with you, Dad! And I'm really excited to be learning about Clara Barton.

Dad: While you're with me learning about Clara Barton, Mom and Tommy are in Europe interviewing Florence Nightingale. She, too, was a famous nurse.

Tammy: Clara Barton was a nurse during the Civil War, right? People called her the "Angel of the Battlefield."

Dad: That's true. But she did a lot more than that to help people. I'm most interested in how she helped found the American Red Cross. Why don't we start there with our interviews?

Tammy: But Dad, I want to find out what Clara was like when she was my age. Before she grew up and became famous.

Dad: Okay, then. Let's start on her family farm in North Oxford, Massachusetts. Please set the *When Machine* to 1833.

Tammy: Great, Dad. It's all set. What will we find there?

Dad: Although Clara is only 11, she's already taking care of people. A few weeks ago, her brother David fell from a roof and hurt himself. Let's see how he's doing.

Tammy: Here we are in 1833!

Dad: And there are Clara and David.

Clara Barton: Angel of the Battlefield
(Excerpt 2)

David: I know. She helps me with everything. She's promised to take care of me until I'm well. How's that for a sister?

Tammy: Clara, are you thinking about becoming a nurse when you grow up?

Clara: My father wants me to become a teacher.

David: She's very smart and has been reading since she was 4. But I think she should become a nurse. She's so kind to everyone.

Dad: You're right, David. But Clara will find that out for herself. Well, we have to go. Feel better, David. And enjoy this beautiful day. Good-bye, children!

Clara and David: Good-bye!

Tammy: Dad, Clara hardly said anything.

Dad: I know, Tammy. I have read that she was painfully shy as a child. But as a woman she wasn't afraid of anything. I want to see how she changed. I'm setting the *When Machine* for 1865. Let's visit her then.

Tammy: Did David get better?

Dad: Yes, he did. Clara nursed him for two years while he recovered from the injury.

Unit 7

Table of Contents

From the Poem "Paul Revere's Ride"

PAUL REVERE'S RIDE, APRIL 18, 1775.

Henry Wadsworth Longfellow wrote the famous poem "Paul Revere's Ride." The poem is set at the time of the American Revolution—1775. The following is an excerpt from that poem.

Listen my children and you shall hear
Of the midnight ride of Paul Revere,
On the eighteenth of April, in Seventy-five;
Hardly a man is now alive
Who remembers that famous day and year.

He said to his friend, "If the British march
By land or sea from the town to-night,
Hang a lantern aloft in the belfry arch
Of the North Church tower as a signal light,—
One if by land, and two if by sea;
And I on the opposite shore will be,
Ready to ride and spread the alarm
Through every Middlesex village and farm,
For the country folk to be up and to arm."

The World's Oceans

Ocean water covers approximately three-quarters of Earth. The oceans make up about ninety-seven percent of the total water on Earth. Humans, animals, and plants depend on the oceans to live.

During a powerful storm at sea, oil tankers can break apart. When this happens, oil spills out and forms a thick blanket on the water. Within hours, oil covers nearby plants and wildlife.

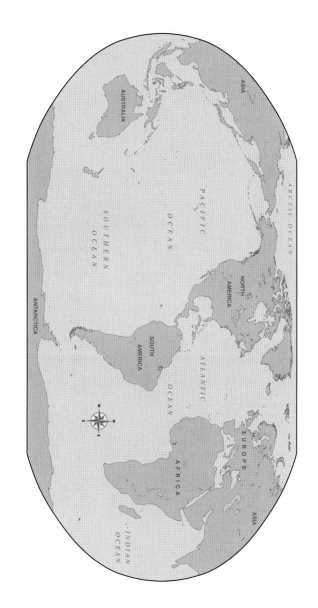

The spill has polluted clean water and caused huge changes. The area won't be clean again for months, or even years.

Toxic wastes such as chemicals and fertilizers can cause damage, too. When toxic waste gets into the ground, rain washes it deep into the earth. Streams underground carry toxic waste into creeks and rivers, and finally into the oceans.

Nuclear Energy

Nuclear energy comes from uranium. Uranium is a metal. Splitting atoms in pellets of uranium into much smaller parts releases a huge amount of energy. This energy can generate electricity. Around the world more than 400 nuclear power plants are generating electricity.

Nuclear energy costs much less than energy from fossil fuels, such as coal and oil. Nuclear energy also leads to less air pollution. Nuclear energy helps meet our growing demand for electricity.

The process of releasing nuclear energy creates radioactive waste. The used uranium pellets, and the containers in which they are stored, give off harmful radiation. Large amounts of radiation can cause cancer and even death. The pellets and containers continue to release radioactive waste for hundreds of thousands of years.

Mystery of the Missing Raffle Ticket

Dustin exploded into the house, slamming the door. He startled his parrot, Molly, who flew to the security of her cage.

"What's the emergency, Dusty?" called his sister, Alicia.

"I won the school raffle," shouted Dustin. "When I redeem my ticket, I get center-ice seats to the Blackhawks!"

Dustin and Alicia raced into his bedroom to get the ticket he had pinned to his bulletin board. But when they got there, it was gone.

"WHAT?" screamed Dustin. "We've got to find that ticket. It was pinned up, so Mom couldn't have tossed it by accident when she cleaned."

"Maybe one of your friends took it," suggested Alicia.

"My friends wouldn't do that!" said Dustin.

"Sorry," said Alicia. "Plus, it's not like anyone knew you would win, *and* claiming the prize would expose the thief."

The siblings searched but couldn't find the ticket. "I bet it somehow fell on the floor and Mom *did* get rid of it without realizing," concluded Alicia.

Dustin paced, unconvinced, but with no better theory. Suddenly he spotted his ticket in the bottom of Molly's cage! "There it is," he shouted.

"She must have taken it during one of her flights around the house," Alicia said.

"Molly wants to see the Blackhawks," Dustin said, laughing. "You wacky parrot, they're not actually other birds!"

Mystery of the Creaking Stairs

I'm a pretty cool guy, but it creeped me out that the basement stairs creaked whenever my parents were out for the evening. They'd go out the door between the house and garage, get in the car, and drive off. Within minutes, the noise would start. It didn't bother my older brother, Calvin, but not much penetrated his brain when he was reading. Once he asked if I had acousticophobia. Only a first-degree bookworm would know a crazy, complicated word for "fear of noise."

I wasn't afraid of the noise, just what was *making* it. I was convinced it was a ghost, but Calvin thought that idea was hilarious (though he used the word *risible*). Finally, one night I made Calvin put down his book and come with me to the basement. I grabbed Mom's cast-iron skillet and handed Calvin the broom.

We turned on the basement lights and a whole family of raccoons blinked at us. They bolted up the stairs, charged through the door to the garage, and squeezed through a hole at the bottom of the garage door.

"Mystery solved, Sherlock," said Calvin.

He was right. The only time that door was open was when we went somewhere in the car, and from the look of things in the basement, that's when the raccoons helped themselves to food we kept there. Case—and door—closed.

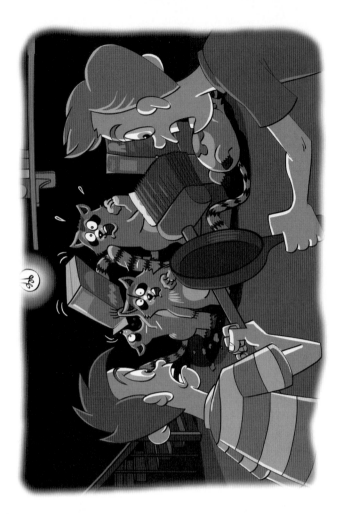

Runt Takes the Cake

CHAPTER ONE

"Get the lead out, Runtowski!" Mr. Nordmann, our phys ed teacher shook the rope that Runt was climbing. Runt lost his grip and fell. The class gasped. Runt landed on the mat, somersaulted into a standing position and took a bow, turning the gasps to laughter. Nordmann muttered something under his breath and said to Runt, "Drop and give me twenty." To us he said, "And that goes for the rest of you ladies, too."

Nordmann was telling us what a flabby bunch of wissies we were when he fell silent. We looked up in the middle of push-up number fifteen to see him clutch his chest, turn purple, and fall facedown on the hardwood floor.

We all stood there in shock while Runt felt Nordmann's neck for a pulse.

"Who has a cell phone?" he asked.

We were all in our gym shorts. No one had one. Runt reached into Nordmann's pocket, yanked out his cell, and dialed 9-1-1.

"He's not breathing," I said. Runt and I tried rolling the bodybuilder onto his back, but we were Chihuahuas trying to budge a beached whale. It took six ginormous guys to roll Nordmann over so Runt could try CPR. It wasn't perfect, but he got Nordmann breathing.

The first paramedics to arrive shoved Runt out of the way, put Nordmann on oxygen, hoisted him onto the gurney, and wheeled him out to the waiting ambulance. The rest of the class followed, leaving Runt and me staring after them.

"You're welcome," Runt said to no one in particular.

CHAPTER TWO

Mr. Nordmann died of cardiac arrest before the ambulance got to the hospital, which surprised Runt, given Nordmann's superb physical condition. "Had to be foul play," he mused as we fought our way through the crowd at the cemetery to pay our respects on this foggy February day.

Humongous mourners—former football players whom Mr. Nordmann had coached over the years—huddled 'round the coffin. We couldn't penetrate the offensive line to reach the graveside and were getting bored. Runt nudged me and whispered, "Look over your shoulder." I turned.

There stood Mr. Sloathe, our biology teacher, the school's hardest grader, widely known—and hated—as The Flunkinator.

Rumor had it that Nordmann and Sloathe had had a nasty confrontation when Sloathe failed Nordmann's star halfback, disqualifying him before the league championship. Some kids said they had come to blows, but I doubt that. Nordmann could have pounded the tall but muscle-free Sloathe into library paste.

"What's Sloathe smirking about?" I wondered aloud.

"Not him," Runt whispered, pointing to a figure farther away, "her."

A tall woman lurked behind a tree. Her black veil obscured a bony, chalk-white face, dark eyebrows, and blood-red lips. Her luminous skin sucked all the light out of the day.

The next day in the cafeteria, a moody Runt picked at his food. To cheer him up I said, "Eat, bro. It may be barfeteria slop, but for some reason, it's tasty." It was true. Lately, the food here was scrumptious. Nobody brought their own lunch anymore. Even teachers were standing in line. Having hairnetted ladies serve you food you actually enjoyed was like experiencing a total eclipse of the sun.

"Ith thooo good," I said, showing him the gross wad of chewed chicken casserole in my mouth. "Don't you want to grow up to be big and throng like me?" I teased.

Runt ignored me. "That lady we saw yesterday. I've seen her before," he said.

"Yeah, she seemed familiar, but I'm drawing a blank." Runt brightened. "That's it! The Blanc fire!"

"Half the town was at the Blanc fire last month," I reminded him. Runt and I had suffered in Mr. Blanc's English class, but his horrific end was undeserved. You could see the blaze from Space Station 1.

"Wait a minute, you're right." My memory flashed on a woman at the edge of the crowd, her black eyes fixed on the fire. Her bone-white face was hard to miss, even in the dark.

"Sloathe was there that night as well," I said. "He and Blanc didn't exactly get along, either. I once had to take a message to the teacher's lounge and walked in on the middle of a shouting match."

"Really?" I had Runt's interest now. I actually knew something Runt didn't. I savored this rare moment.

"Yeah. Blanc had called him a 'dolphin killer.' They were having some kind of fight over animal rights."

"Interesting," Runt said. "Sloathe fights with two teachers; two teachers die."

CHAPTER THREE

It was early morning as we navigated the twisted corridors of Bellmore High's subterranean service areas. Inquiring minds demanded to know the source of the cafeteria's culinary excellence. The school paper's editor assigned its star reporter (me) to interview chef Clarissa Nicir. I had cajoled Runt into coming along to be my photographer.

"Why did we have to come here before school?" he grumbled.

"Because it's the only time she would agree to the interview. Principal Lattimer had to beg her to talk to us," I replied.

Ms. Nicir was bent over a sink rinsing pots in the kitchen. As I set up my recorder on a table I said, "I'm Eddie Steadman from the Bellmore Bellringer. Your fans want to know all about you."

Runt and I were gawking at our chalk-white lady! I managed to return my jaw to a closed position and stammered, "Um . . . we're in awe of your culinary genius. That chicken at lunch yesterday was superb! Can the students expect more of the same?"

Clarissa Nicir turned out to be very nice, but Runt took only a few shots of her during our interview. He spent way too much time shooting utensils and cupboards. It turns out that Ms. Nicir had switched careers from nursing to cooking. She studied at a prestigious cooking school in France but turned down offers from five-star restaurants to work here. When I asked her why, she said she wanted to use her expertise to improve the quality of Bellmore's education by raising the quality of the cuisine.

"Good nutrition feeds your brain," she smiled. "Speaking of brains, I need someone to take this chocolate cake to Mr. Sloathe." When she saw the puzzled look on my face she said, "I'm afraid Mr. Sloathe and I had a bit of a misunderstanding recently. Since it's his birthday, I thought this cake would help patch things up."

I almost told her that the cake might just save her life, but kept my mouth shut. All Runt and I had were half-baked theories, no pun intended.

Runt volunteered to deliver the treat and then the bell rang for first period.

"Really? Why me?" Ms. Nicir put the pot in the dishwasher and turned to face us.

©2014 Benchmark Education Company, LLC

CHAPTER FOUR

By the time I got out of band practice, it was already getting dark. I took the shortcut through the parking lot and was rounding the side of a delivery truck parked behind the cafeteria when a bony hand grabbed my arm.

"Your little friend never delivered my cake." Ms. Nicir's livid face loomed out of the shadows. She was trying to smile, but I could see panic in her eyes.

"Oh, hey, Ms. Nicir," I said. "He probably just forgot about it and left it in his locker."

"He better not have touched it," she cooed. "That was specially prepared for Mr. Sloathe."

"I'll find out what happened to it," I said. Her talons were digging into my arm.

"Here's my number." She thrust a piece of paper into my hands, "Call me as soon as you find out anything." She ran off toward her car.

As I walked into the oncoming darkness, I blamed the wind for sending icy fingers down my spine. Home was across town, a jillion miles away, and I was alone. Then something lurched at me from behind a tree.

"Eddie," it said.

"Yah!" I screamed, trying to sound less like a terrified five-year-old girl when I saw it was Runt by adding, "where's Nicir's cake? She's about to string you up."

"It's where it should be," he said calmly, "at the crime lab. It was poisoned."

Runt had been a busy busybody that day. Before school started, he called his dad about his suspicions about Ms. Nicir. Detective Runtowski refused to waste police department resources to follow up on his son's wild hunch, but he had a suggestion. Mr. Sloathe was a scientist. Why not have him run the test himself? Mr. Sloathe rose to the challenge and discovered the cake contained high levels of succinylcholine, a drug that can cause cardiac arrest.

"You can only get it in hospitals," Runt explained. "Nicir would have had access to the stuff from her days as a nurse."

"What tipped you off?" I asked.

"This," he said, whipping out his digital camera and clicking to those kitchen cupboard shots. Runt had pushed aside the usual cooking ingredients so the camera could capture the collection of poisons hidden in the back.

"The gourmet food was just bait to get the teachers to start eating at the cafeteria."

"That would explain why Mr. Nordmann, the triathlete, died of a heart attack," I said.

"Dad's going to order an autopsy on Mr. Blanc, too. He was in that blaze, but there isn't any smoke in his lungs. I'll bet there isn't any smoke in his lungs. I'm thinking she poisoned him, then started the fire."

"Okay," I conceded, "but why?"

"Dad finally got interested when Sloathe found the poison, so he ran the fingerprints on the cake box. The database search produced someone who looked like Ms. Nicir, only the name was Velma Montez."

"That name sounds familiar," I said.

"My oldest brother, Ryan, remembered her son, Ray Montez," Runt said. "He dropped out of school and eventually wound up in prison. Could be Mrs. Montez blamed the teachers."

I grimaced. "I hope you're wrong."

"Why's that?"

"Because if they put Nicir away, we're back to cafeteria food as usual."

©2014 Benchmark Education Company, LLC

Reread the Mystery

Analyze the Characters and Plot

- Who are the main characters in this mystery?
- Who are the minor characters?
- What purpose do the minor characters serve?
- What is the problem in this mystery?
- Who killed Mr. Nordmann and Mr. Blanc? Why were they killed?
- How does the mystery end?

Focus on Comprehension: Author's Purpose

- What is the author's purpose for writing this mystery?
- Murder is a serious subject, yet the author included several moments of humor. For what purpose did the author include humor?
- Why did the author organize this story into chapters?

Focus on Red Herrings

Red herrings are distractions or diversions used by good mystery writers. They are intended to confuse the reader and lead them away from the real criminal. Until the very end of the story when Runt explains that he thinks the chef did it, whom did you think killed Mr. Nordmann and Mr. Blanc? What red herrings did the author include that led you away from Clarissa Nicir?

Analyze the Tools Writers Use: Hyperbole

- On page 101, the author, through Eddie's narration, says that the phys ed students were Chihuahuas trying to budge a beached whale. What type of comparison is the hyperbole making?
- On page 102, the author talks about Mr. Nordmann pounding Mr. Sloathe into library paste. Explain how this is a hyperbole.
- On page 103, the author says that Mr. Blanc's house-fire blaze could be seen from Space Station 1. How does this hyperbole describe the fire's blaze?
- On page 105, Eddie is walking home and realizes that home is a jillion miles away. How does this hyperbole show his nervousness?

Focus on Words: Portmanteau

Make a chart like the one below. Use a dictionary or the Internet to determine each portmanteau word's definition, the words it is based on, and its origin. (Note that some of the words were invented by the author.)

Page	Word	Definition	Words It Is Based On	Origin and When Word Was First Used
101	wissies			
101	ginormous			
102	humongous			
103	barfeteria			
103	grumbled			

Hurricanes

Every year, from June to November, hurricanes sweep out of the Gulf of Mexico, the Caribbean Sea, and the warm parts of the Atlantic Ocean. When viewed from outer space, hurricanes look like small, flat spirals drifting on the water. Up close, however, they can be quite destructive.

Hurricane winds can reach speeds of 200 miles (322 kilometers) per hour and more. Their winds are powerful enough to tear apart small buildings. They also bring heavy rains, which can lead to serious flooding.

A hurricane's clouds may rise 10,000 feet (3,048 meters) high and cover thousands of square miles. Its clouds, winds, and rain rotate around a center, or eye, like a gigantic top. The eye itself is calm, but the winds just beyond it are very powerful. Even 300 miles (483 kilometers) from the eye, the winds of a hurricane may still be 60 miles (97 kilometers) per hour.

Along the Atlantic and Gulf coasts, hurricanes generally travel west and north in a curved path. A hurricane usually moves 20 to 30 miles (32 to 48 kilometers) per hour, but it can go much faster. Hurricanes can also travel thousands of miles (kilometers). Even New England can be hit by these tropical storms. As a rule, though, a hurricane loses force and begins to die out as it moves north and over land.

Sleepless Beauty (Excerpt 1)

Beauty: Let me see what is on my To-Do List for this week. (*reading list*) One: Put the cans, bottles, and spices in order by size. Two: Learn French. Three: Read the dictionary . . . again.

King: Beauty, your mother and I want to talk with you.

Queen: You know how we worry, dear. You haven't slept since you turned sixteen.

King: You're twenty now!

Queen: That's *four years* without a decent night's sleep!

Beauty: Yes, I know. It really is tiresome. Well, not really tiresome, of course, because I never actually get tired.

Queen: We know, dear. That's why your father has come up with a plan. Tell her, Earnest.

King: Beauty, I've had posters put up everywhere. They say that you will marry the first prince who can put you to sleep. You can always say no, but—

Beauty: How can I say no? I do so miss dreaming!

Queen: Well, that's a relief, because we have three

princes waiting in the outer hall. Prime Minister Prudence, please bring in the first prince!

Prudence: (*announcing*) It is my honor to present Prince Dishwater, from the kingdom of Dulluz!

Prince Dishwater: Well, would you look at that! This is quite a large room, isn't it? I believe it's larger than our throne room, but perhaps not quite so large as my uncle's throne room. Although now that I look closer—

King: Excuse me, Prince Dishwater. My wife and I would just like to know: Why do you think you can help our daughter sleep?

Prince Dishwater: (*to himself*) Did I see a parrot in a cage in the outer room? I'd swear it was a palm cockatoo . . . (*louder*) Oh, sorry, your majesty. Did you ask why I thought I should marry your daughter? Well, you see, I'm often told that I have a gift for putting people to sleep. I'm not exactly sure how I do this.

Beauty: (*softly*) I can guess.

Sleepless Beauty (Excerpt 2)

Beauty: (*annoyed*) It's so what?

Prince Dreamy: Ahhhhhh, and this is the dazzling Beauty. Your name brings to mind a tranquil beach . . . under a soft blue sky . . . with the waves gently lapping against the shore . . .

King, Queen, and Prudence: (*snoring*) Zzzzzzzzz . . .

Beauty: (*claps*) Wake up! Wake up! This isn't working for me!

Prince Dreamy: Now, now, now. I think somebody should go to her peaceful place and relax—

Prudence: If you will just follow me out please, Prince Dreamy.

Prince Dreamy: Perhaps I can help *you* find your peaceful place, Prime Minister.

Prudence: I don't think that would be advisable.

Prince Dreamy: (*trailing off*) Just close your eyes and picture yourself in a charming green meadow . . . the birds are warbling . . . tweet . . . tweet . . .

Sir Lock-Homes: Excuse me? Hello? Sorry to barge in like this, but your prime minister is busy with some man who's tweeting at her.

King: Oh, do come in, Prince—

Sir Lock-Homes: Actually, I'm not a prince, your majesty. I'm a duke. Here is my card.

Queen: (*reading card*) Sir Lock-Homes, Duke of Doyle, Problems Solved and Solutions Found.

Beauty: Are you a detective?

Unit 8

Table of Contents

Some Weather

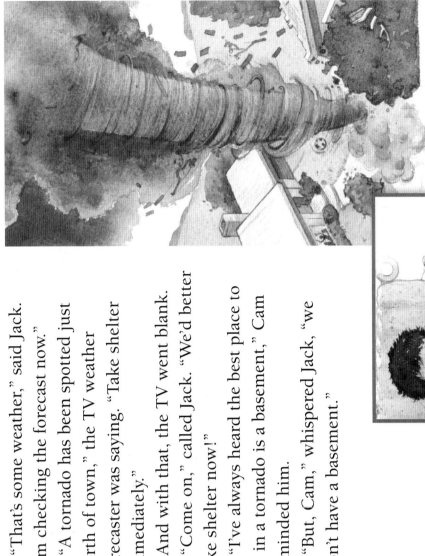

Cam was just finishing her homework when her brother Jack came into the room.

"Hey, Cam," Jack said, "Look out the window. Did you ever see clouds that black?"

"And look at the neighbors' trees," Cam added. "The wind is blowing so hard that they're almost touching the ground."

Just as Cam spoke, hailstones as large as golf balls began to clatter to the ground.

"That's some weather," said Jack. "I'm checking the forecast now."

"A tornado has been spotted just north of town," the TV weather forecaster was saying. "Take shelter immediately."

And with that, the TV went blank.

"Come on," called Jack. "We'd better take shelter now!"

"I've always heard the best place to go in a tornado is a basement," Cam reminded him.

"But, Cam," whispered Jack, "we don't have a basement."

Cheap Land!

In the late 1800s, railroad companies in the United States put up thousands of posters to entice people to move west.

RICH FARMING LANDS!

ON THE LINE OF THE

UNION PACIFIC RAILROAD!

Located in the GREAT CENTRAL BELT of POPULATION, COMMERCE and WEALTH, and adjoining the WORLD'S HIGHWAY from OCEAN TO OCEAN.

12,000,000 ACRES!

3,000,000 Acres in Central and Eastern Nebraska, in the Platte Valley, now for sale!

We invite the attention of all parties seeking a HOME, to the LANDS offered for sale by this Company.

The Vast Quantity of Land from which to select, enables every one to secure such a location as he desires, suitable to any branch of farming or stock raising.

The Prices are Extremely Low. The amount of land owned by the Company is so large that they are enabled to sell at the cheapest possible rates, ranging from $ per acre.

feed with avidity and fatten upon the nutritious grasses without grain; hogs thrive well, and wool growing is exceedingly remunerative.

Timber is found on the streams and grows rapidly.

Coal of excellent quality, exists in vast quantities along the road in Wyoming, and in the line the

Bacteria

Bacteria are single-celled organisms. There are three shapes of bacteria: round, rod, and spiral.

Some bacteria are harmful to humans. Have you ever had strep throat or an ear infection? If so, bacteria had invaded your body.

The inside of a human body is warm and moist—an excellent place for bacteria to grow.

Most of the time your white blood cells are able to kill harmful bacteria in your body. But sometimes there are too many bacteria to kill. You might have to take antibiotics, medicines that kill bacteria.

Some bacteria become resistant to antibiotics. This means the antibiotics can no longer kill the bacteria. Scientists constantly work to find new antibiotics to kill bacteria.

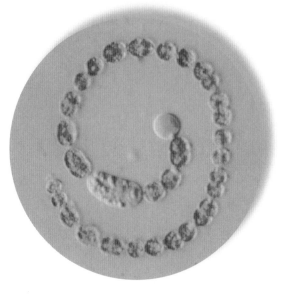

spiral bacteria

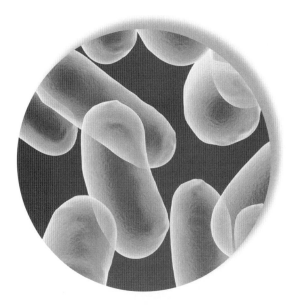

rod-shaped bacteria

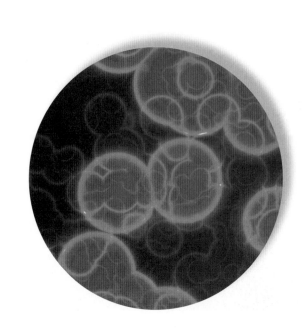

round bacteria

Campout Cop-Out

Cast: Three thirteen-year-old boys, Rajah, Matthew, Kimio

Setting: Night. Kimio's backyard, surrounded by woods. Tents are up, boys are sitting around a lit flashlight.

Rajah: Man, it's really quiet here.

Kimio: Yeah, sometimes it gets really boring, though, so I'm happy you guys came for a campout sleepover tonight.

Matthew: How can you possibly get bored exploring the woods all summer?

Kimio: You'd be surprised, but I'm just saying it's not great living so far from everyone.

The boys eat marshmallows from a bag. Suddenly they hear twigs and leaves crunching loudly in the woods.

Rajah: (*nervous*) Er, what the heck is that? It's not a bear, is it?

Kimio: Nah, I've heard there are black bears somewhere out there, but no one's ever seen any.

The sounds get louder; sound closer.

Matthew: (*worried, voice rising*) Yeah, but have you ever been out here in the dark before with a bag of marshmallows?

Kimio: Good point. Let's go!

The sounds are really close and loud now. The boys get up, grab the marshmallows, forget the flashlight, and run toward Kimio's house. None of them glance backward so they don't see the squirrel emerge from the woods in the beam of the flashlight.

Invitation Upset

Cast: Three fifth-grade girls, Sunita, Nilda, Caroline

Setting: School lunchroom table

Sunita: I'm totally excited about Indra's birthday party Saturday—it should be great!

Nilda: Party? I know her birthday's coming, but I haven't gotten any invitation. When did you?

Caroline: They were peeking out of our desks this morning. I haven't opened mine yet, but I know from how my name is written in glitter that it's from Indra.

Sunita: You know she gets really into things and likes being the queen of surprises, sneaking invitations into desks this time, backpacks last time. Just check your desk later.

Nilda: I rummaged around in it this morning, looking for my eraser, and there's no invitation.

Sunita: Don't be upset. I'm sure it's a mistake, 'cause you know she always invites all of us. Why wouldn't she invite you?

Nilda: *(concerned)* She's been acting weird with me since I beat her in that track meet and upset her winning record.

Sunita: Nah, she's not like that.

Caroline pulls out her invitation. A second one drops to the table. It has Nilda's name on it. The girls react with surprise.

Nilda: *(relieved)* It must have gotten stuck to the glitter glue!

Caroline: *(smiling)* Let's open them together!

New Kid in School

Cast of Characters

PAT: An eleven-year-old boy

ALDO: An eleven-year-old boy

Setting

An elementary school classroom, a little before lunch

(Lights up on a school classroom. PAT and ALDO sit in chair-desks, with an armrest for writing. They are in separate rows. The lighting shifts to a spotlight on just PAT when he is talking and just ALDO when he is talking. PAT and ALDO are voicing interior monologues—their thoughts. They do not hear each other.)

PAT: That new kid here sure is weird. His family comes from a different country or something, and he doesn't speak English well. The teacher treats him like royalty or something. She says he's really smart and we should welcome him, and learn from him, and blah, blah, blah. But I don't know what I can learn from somebody I can hardly understand.

ALDO: It's hard to know the right thing to do. This new student in class—he looks different from the rest of us, and he's very shy. And nobody talks to him. He always eats lunch by himself. I feel bad for him. Should I talk to him, or not? I'm sitting on the fence.

PAT: Things were going pretty good in class until that new kid came along, right in the middle of the year. The teacher is always stopping to make sure he understands what she's talking about. What a waste of time.

ALDO: It must be hard for that new kid. A new country and language and all. He works very hard to keep up with us. The teacher says he studies night and day. If I had to go to school in another country where they speak a different language, I would be totally at sea.

PAT: I can't even remember the kid's name. Oh, yeah, it's Simo. Simo? What kind of a name is that? Definitely weird.

ALDO: Simo is his name. I've never heard of that name before. Sounds interesting. I wonder what the name means.

PAT: Everybody already has their friends. Who wants to be friends with him? Maybe they'll switch him to another class. Then things will be back to normal.

ALDO: I know that some of the other kids in the class are keeping away from him just because he's different. But being different isn't a bad thing. If I went to another country, I would be the one who's different, right?

PAT: All I can say is I'm not going to deal with him. Who needs the hassle?

ALDO: I think it would be interesting to find out what it's like where he comes from. Maybe I'll ask him to sit with me at lunch. I'll be going out on a limb, I know. Some of my friends might think I'm weird, too.

PAT: Aldo keeps looking at that new kid. I bet he's going to go talk to Simo. The weirdo.

ALDO: I absolutely will eat lunch with him. I bet he'll like that. Who cares what the others think.

(The lunch bell rings. The lights shift to show the full classroom. ALDO and PAT get up from their seats, and begin putting their books and papers away.)

PAT: *(calling out)* Hey, Aldo, you coming with us to lunch?

ALDO: Not today, Pat, I've got other plans. *(calling out)* Hey, Simo, wait up!

(Lights fade out as ALDO exits hastily, leaving PAT onstage, alone, thinking.)

THE END

Reread the Play

Analyze the Characters and Plot

- Who are the characters in the play?
- Where does the play take place?
- What is the main problem in the play?
- Is the problem resolved?
- What happens at the end of the play?

Analyze the Tools Writers Use: Idioms

- What does Aldo mean when he says on page 117 that he is sitting on the fence?
- On page 117, Aldo says that the new kid studies night and day. How can that be? What does this idiom really mean?
- Aldo is "going out on a limb" (page 118) to eat with the new kid. What does he mean by that?

Focus on Words: Descriptive Language (Adjectives and Adverbs)

Authors use adjectives and adverbs to help readers connect with a story. Authors use adjectives to help readers see, feel, smell, touch, and taste the written word. Authors use adverbs to describe how, where, when, and how often characters act. Make a chart like the one below. Read each descriptive word. Tell if it is an adjective or an adverb, and then explain what is describes.

Page	Word	Adjective or Adverb	What It Describes
117	weird		
117	different		
117	hardly		
117	shy		
118	already		
118	absolutely		

Leave It to Smart

It was only after her guests had gone that Estella realized that her new jeweled ball with the diamond bird inside was missing. Just two hours before, a few of her friends had come by to see the beautiful little trinket. Before showing it to them, Estella served refreshments in the living room. After admiring the lovely ball and chatting awhile, Stan and Lulu had left together. Penny had left soon after, saying she had to get to the library before it closed. Immediately after Estella discovered that the ball was missing, she called Inspector Smart.

Inspector Smart left Estella's house smiling; he had solved the mystery. When he had arrived at her house, he searched the living room first. "Who was the last person in the room?" he asked. After a moment's thought, Estella conceded, "I was." Smart pointed to the cat playing under the piano with a small object. "What about the cat?" Estella rushed over to the piano, exclaiming, "She came in as I was going out!" As Estella picked up her priceless ball and smiled widely, Inspector Smart said, "Not even a good cat can pass up a diamond bird."

The Lion and the Mouse Shoot Hoops (Excerpt 1)

Narrator: This tale is about a group of sixth grade kids who liked to play basketball. Anna, Ricardo, and Jade were pretty good players, but the best of all was Leona Lyle, whose nickname was Lion. Lion was great—the only problem was that sometimes she hogged the ball.

Ricardo: Lion, why don't you let me have the ball once in a while?

Leona: Because you're never open. Besides, we're winning—what else could you want?

Ricardo: I'd like to do something besides stand around and watch you score.

Leona: I'm not going to try to pass to you if the other team might steal the ball.

Jade: Are you kidding? We never steal the ball!

Anna: It's not fun when the game is this lopsided.

Leona: I'm not having fun because it's too easy. Why don't we switch around: you three against me?

Ricardo: Fine with me. At least the rest of us might finally get a chance to take some shots.

Narrator: Even with three people against her, Lion won easily.

Leona: Too bad we can't make it four against me, because I need more of a challenge.

Narrator: Just as Lion spoke, a tiny kid came onto the court. In a squeaky little voice he said:

Marvin: Hi, everybody. I'm Marvin. Can I play, too?

Jade: No, little dude, you can't. You're too small and you might get squished. Besides, anybody as tiny as you can't possibly be any good at basketball.

Marvin: I know I'm not very good, but if you give me the ball, I'll show you one thing I can do.

Leona: Come on, Jade, let's see his stuff. Here, kid—catch!

Marvin: Oof! Hey, you don't have to throw it so hard!

The Lion and the Mouse Shoot Hoops (Excerpt 2)

Big Mouth: The Lord of the Rims steals the ball from Pip-squeak Number One! He's down the court and nobody can get near him . . . He shoots, he scores, and the crowd goes wild!

Narrator: The ninth graders quickly saw that Lion was the only player to worry about. They ignored her teammates and covered her closely. Lion fought hard. She managed to make some baskets, but the ninth graders were bigger and better. They scored . . . .

Stilts: Ha! Two points!

Narrator: . . . and scored . . . .

Turbo: Woo-hoo! Check out my turnaround jump shot! I hope you kids are taking notes.

Narrator: . . . and scored.

Big Mouth: I'm the Pharaoh of the Free Throw! Bow in awe of my titanic talent, then kneel at my feet and call me Sir Score-a-lot!

Anna: Will you stop talking? You're driving me crazy!

Narrator: Lion played her hardest. Soon the game was tied, eight to eight. The next team to make a basket would win. The players took time out to huddle and refine their strategies. On one side of the court, the ninth graders were laughing and joking. They hadn't even broken a sweat.

Stilts: I'm ready to win and get those sixth graders out of the way.

Big Mouth: The Dean of Demolition is ready to blast them off the court!

Turbo: As long as we keep that Leona girl covered, we're fine. She's actually very good. I still haven't figured out whether that tiny kid who looks like a rodent is actually playing. He doesn't do anything except stand in the middle of the court and squeak when I run by.

Narrator: On the other side of the court, Lion and her friends knew they were in trouble.

Anna: Big Mouth keeps faking me out and darting around me.

Jade: I can't keep Turbo covered because she's so fast—I blink my eyes and she's halfway to the basket!

Unit 9

Table of Contents

Disappearing Forests

Forests disappear for many reasons. Wildfires burn hundreds of thousands of trees around the world every year. Powerful storms can rip up trees by their roots. People cut down and burn trees to prepare land for farming and ranching, or to make way for new homes and roads.

Today, the most rapid deforestation, or loss of forests, takes place in tropical rain forests. Thousands of square miles of South America's Amazon rain forest are cleared each year for farms, ranches, homes, and roads.

Deforestation is dramatically changing Earth's landscapes, and not in a good way. Protecting the world's forests is among the most important environmental challenges of this century. Keeping Earth's forests healthy is everybody's job.

Regions of Canada

Canada is the second largest country in the world. It includes many different geographical regions. In the Arctic north are the frozen plains, or tundra. In the southeast is a hilly, rocky region.

Western Canada consists of several geographical regions, too, including wide-open prairies. The prairies are mostly flat, and have very fertile soil. Farther west, the Rocky Mountains rise abruptly, creating a region of towering mountains and dramatic valleys.

One of the most beautiful regions of western Canada is the coast of the Pacific Ocean. The coastal region has the country's wettest and mildest climate. Parts of Vancouver Island, just off Canada's western coast, get as much as 262 inches (665 centimeters) of rain per year! Canada is a country of vastly ranging geographical regions.

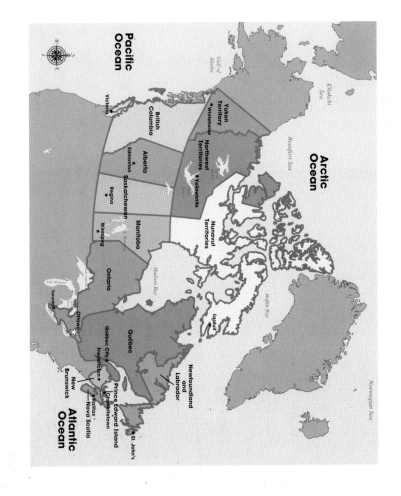

Genes

Genes are tiny cell parts that determine certain traits, such as the shape of your eyes or the color of your hair. Genes determine not only how you look, but how you grow. Genes can affect how healthy you will be, too.

You are born with your genes. It is important that you understand what your genes can and cannot do. You should understand what genes mean to your health, your personality, and how you look.

Scientists are trying to learn more about genes and how they work. Perhaps through research, scientists will be able to control genes, and cure diseases caused by faulty genes.

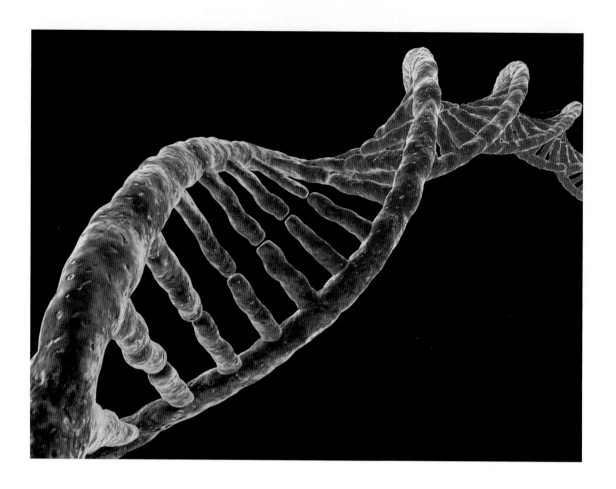

The Wonder of Alice

The book *Alice in Wonderland* by Lewis Carroll begins one afternoon when a white rabbit in a waistcoat rushes past a young girl named Alice. He stops, looks at a pocket watch, and then hurries down a rabbit hole. Alice follows him and finds herself in Wonderland.

Wonderland is an odd place where odd things happen. Alice shrinks and grows depending upon what she's had to eat and drink. Once, she grows so enormous that she fills an entire house! Alice goes to the world's rudest tea party, where she meets the March Hare, the Mad Hatter, and the Dormouse. She argues with a caterpillar and chats with a grinning cat that suddenly appears and disappears. She meets the Queen of Hearts, who uses flamingoes as croquet mallets. Alice finally wakes up back in her own world.

It's easy to see why this classic from 1865 is still enjoyed today. It's a fun fantasy for all ages.

A live-action movie inspired by the book was released in 2010. Also called *Alice in Wonderland*, the movie should please fans of the book even though there are some differences between the two. For one, Alice is nineteen in the movie. Like with the book, the movie's Alice is a bit dull. But it's hard to compete with the likes of Johnny Depp as the Mad Hatter and all that gorgeous scenery.

Because of Winn-Dixie

Ten-year-old Opal Buloni narrates Kate DiCamillo's novel *Because of Winn-Dixie*. The summer Opal and her preacher father move to a new town, Opal is lonely and misses her friends. She also misses her absent mother. Opal goes to the grocery store and comes home with a stray dog she names Winn-Dixie.

Winn-Dixie is a dog that likes to smile. And that makes people smile back. Opal and Winn-Dixie quickly make friends with townspeople, young and old alike.

Opal learns that a lot of folks can feel melancholy. Everyone has some sadness, and friends can help you feel better. By the novel's end, Opal also realizes she has a lot to be thankful for.

This novel, published in 2000, is wonderful, gentle in tone, serious, thoughtful, and funny. The laughing, lovable friendship between Opal and Winn-Dixie is the story's heart. Thanks to Opal and Winn-Dixie, readers learn to look beneath the surface to really know a person (or dog). This is a MUST read.

In 2005, the book became a movie. The filmmakers did a great job bringing the characters and setting to life. AnnaSophia Robb is perfect as Opal. But there are some changes and new scenes. The new material has some mean-spiritedness to it that takes away from the book's lovely, sweet world. The movie is good. The book is better.

Star Wars: A New Hope
Movie Reviews

Predictable Entertainment

by Cynthia Swain

Star Wars: A New Hope has plenty of action, some fun battle scenes, and nice special effects. But it's just the age-old story of good versus evil set in outer space. You don't have to be a rocket scientist to figure out who is going to win.

You do have to like the good guys. They're part of the Rebel Alliance, a group of people who have a crusade against the Galactic Empire. Luke Skywalker is the main character. He's a brave young man who learns to become a Jedi knight.

His teacher, Obi-Wan Kenobi, makes the supreme sacrifice to save the galaxy. Princess Leia is one of the feisty leaders of the Rebel Alliance who shows a lot of courage. Han Solo starts out caring only about money; however, he proves to be a loyal friend and an excellent pilot.

The bad guys in this movie have the most awesome weapon, the Death Star. It can (and does) destroy an entire planet. Darth Vader is one of the most menacing villains in the history of villains. He appears to be half

machine and half human. He wears a creepy black helmet. He talks with a threatening hiss, and even the way he breathes sounds intimidating.

His soldiers are the stormtroopers. They're supposed to be scary, dressed up in their white metal armor. Despite their superior weapons and numbers, they can't seem to defeat the rebels.

The Creature Cantina scene has funny moments. However, for my taste, too many of the characters border on being silly. Han's copilot is a "Wookiee." His name is Chewbacca. He looks like a giant monkey. The gangster Jabba the Hutt is a big, brown blob. Ponda Baba, who tries to attack Luke, is a green walrus-like being. The wackiest characters are a band of alien musicians. They have big, bald heads and buggy eyes. Little kids might enjoy these characters, but older viewers would just laugh at them because they take away from the action.

It's fun to watch good win in the end, but there are better ways to spend two hours.

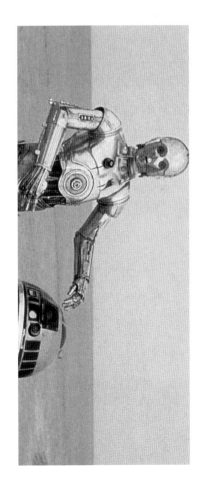

A Blastoff for All by Lucy Forte

Before *Star Wars: A New Hope*, science fiction movies were often slow-moving and cheesy-looking. *Star Wars* changed all that. This film has nonstop action and adventure. In addition, it has the most compelling characters and most dazzling special effects, too. Plus, it's a classic tale about good and evil. Kids and adults can watch this movie over and over and never get tired of it.

As the movie opens, we learn that a galaxy "far, far away" is in a state of civil war. An evil emperor controls the empire with his primary enforcer, Darth Vader. They want to destroy the Rebel Alliance. Only one young farmer can save the galaxy. He lives with his aunt and uncle on a desert planet. His name is Luke Skywalker (played by Mark Hamill).

Luke must learn how to use the Force, a special energy. The Force has been passed on to him from his father, who died as a Jedi knight. Another Jedi, Obi-Wan Kenobi (played by Alec Guinness), a friend of Luke's father, trains Luke in using the Force for good. But watch out: The Force has a dark side! A former Jedi named Darth Vader (the voice of James Earl Jones) went over to the dark side. Now he's one tough opponent. There are other great heroes to help Luke in his battle against the dark side.

In 1977, when *Star Wars: A New Hope* came to theaters, the special effects were considered breathtaking. They still have a big "wow" factor. I got a charge out of the three-dimensional hologram of Princess Leia that R2-D2 has hidden inside his memory system. The Jedi lightsaber is the coolest sword with the neatest sounds.

The battles are flat-out spectacular. Your eyes will open wider than you thought was humanly possible when the Death Star blows apart a planet.

My favorite is the slick pilot Han Solo (played by Harrison Ford). Han Solo risks his life to help Luke. Chewbacca (played by Peter Mayhew), Han's copilot and loyal friend, looks like a 7-foot-tall dog.

Princess Leia (played by Carrie Fisher) is a Rebel leader who handles a laser blaster as well as any man. However, the whining, nervous robot C-3PO (played by Anthony Daniels) did get on my nerves. My favorite character is the smart and cute robot R2-D2 (played by Kenny Baker). Together the heroes make a team that's unbeatable—eventually.

Darth Vader is the ultimate scary bad guy. He is fear personified! He also makes the movie fun to watch, with his horrible helmet, armor, and long robes (all black). The deep, powerful voice of the talented Mr. Jones helps make Vader sound like an evil machine. Vader is the cruelest character I've ever seen in a sci-fi movie. In one scene, he uses his mind (and the Force) to choke one of his own men.

There's also plenty of exciting action. Luke struggles with the lightsaber. Han kills a bounty hunter. Han's ship is captured by the Death Star. Obi-Wan and Darth Vader fight a duel to the death. Princess Leia, Luke, and Han shoot their way out of the Death Star.

And wait until the end! When the Rebel ships get ready to attack the Death Star, my pulse was racing.

At the end of the movie, music builds to a high point, and I found myself standing on my feet. (The music works here, but in other scenes it is almost too strong. It can be distracting and take away from the action.)

Luke and other fighters from the Rebel Alliance fly a crucial mission to destroy the Death Star. They must shoot a torpedo to hit one exact spot, but only an amazing pilot can do it. If they succeed, the Death Star will explode.

Will the Rebels destroy the Death Star? Will the Empire's firepower defeat the Rebels? Will Luke be able to use the Force when it counts? What will happen to Darth Vader? Find out by watching the absolutely best science fiction movie ever.

Reread the Movie Reviews

Understand the Reviews

- What does Cynthia Swain think about the film? Does she like it? How can you tell?
- What does Lucy Forte think about the film? Does she like it? How can you tell?
- How do the two critics differ in their evaluation of the characters? Special effects?

Analyze the Tools Writers Use: Writer's Voice

- Reread the first review. How does Cynthia Swain use her voice to tell you that she does not like the film?
- Reread the second review. How does Lucy Forte use her voice to tell you that she likes the film?

Focus on Words: Superlatives

Make a chart like the one below. Analyze the superlatives in the two movie reviews. Then write down the base adjective.

Page	Superlative	Base Adjective
129	most awesome	
129	most menacing	
129	wackiest	
130	most compelling	
130	most dazzling	
131	cruelest	

A Wish Comes True

Ten, nine, eight . . . The shuttle sat atop the rocket on the launch pad. Inside, Martha read the onboard computer as it recorded the steps toward the final countdown.

"Martha! Pull yourself away from that telescope and come down to dinner!" It was her mother's voice calling across the years. Ever since Martha had received a telescope for her tenth birthday, her eyes had been directed toward the stars.

Seven, six, five . . . "Star light, star bright . . ." Martha was standing by the window wishing on the evening star. "What did you wish?" her father asked. "I can tell only part," Martha said.

"I want a telescope so I can really see my wishing star. The other part is a secret."

Four, three . . . "Martha, they're calling your name!" Martha heard her friend Kathy's voice. "You've made it! You're an astronaut!" Her secret wish was closer to coming true.

Two, one . . . The countdown was almost over. "It's happening! It's finally happening!" Martha's heart pounded. "Blastoff!" With a giant roar, the rocket lifted off the pad. Martha was on her way to see her wishing star at last. The secret part of her wish had come true.

Hansel and Gretel: The True Story (Excerpt 1)

Hansel: (*bratty*) We get to go first.

Gretel: (*bratty*) Yeah, we won the coin toss backstage, remember?

Tina: Yes, I remember. Go ahead and tell our studio audience what happened.

Gretel: Well, we were out in the woods—

Hansel: —working on our merit badges for nature conservation!

Mindy: Merit badges? When did you kids join the scouts?

Gretel: Um . . . a while ago. Anyway, we came upon this strange house made of candy and gingerbread.

Hansel: You could tell its whole purpose was to lure innocent, unsuspecting children like us to it.

Esmerelda: What? Ridiculous!

Tina: You'll have an opportunity to tell your side of the story after Hansel and Gretel finish their side, Esmerelda. Now, go on, kids. Tell us what happened when you arrived at the gingerbread house.

Gretel: We were just standing there admiring the pretty house. All of a sudden, that scary witch over there came out on the porch.

Hansel: She had on a black robe and a pointy black hat, and when she smiled she was missing a bunch of teeth.

Esmerelda: Preposterous! I don't have a black robe or hat, and I assure you I'm not missing any teeth. Look at my smile.

Gretel: Daddy, make her stop interrupting us!

Charles: Excuse me, Tina. I thought that each side gets to tell its version of events without interruption.

Tina: Yes, that is the rule. Esmerelda, I'll have to ask you again to please let the children finish their story.

Esmerelda: I'm sorry. I just want to make sure the audience knows that these children are LYING!

Hansel: We're not lying! We NEVER lie!

Gretel: Yeah! She probably went to the dentist and got her teeth fixed!

Hansel and Gretel: The True Story (Excerpt 2)

Mindy: (gasps) What horrible children to make up such a story!

Charles: Watch what you say about my darling children, Mindy.

Esmerelda: I told them they were welcome to stay with me. I have a spare room, and I thought perhaps they could help me with my work.

Tina: What kind of work do you do?

Esmerelda: I'm a gingerbread-ologist.

Tina: A what?

Esmerelda: A gingerbread-ologist. I study gingerbread. It's one of the most useful substances known. It can be used as food, of course, but also as medicine and as a building material.

Mindy: Your house is really made of gingerbread?

Esmerelda: That's one thing the children got right. It's probably the only thing they got right.

Tina: What were the children doing in your home for three days?

Esmerelda: Mostly getting into trouble. I have never seen such out-of-control children! They climbed on my counters, overturned furniture, and threw my cookie sheets around. I asked them to calm down and they laughed. But the worst thing was when they started eating my house! So, I told them they had to leave. I felt bad that they had no place to go, but I couldn't have them in my home any longer. I simply couldn't tolerate it!

Mindy: I hate to tell you this, darling, but what Esmerelda is saying doesn't sound so farfetched to me.

Charles: WHAT?

Mindy: Listen, I love Hansel and Gretel as if they were my own children. But there's something you need to know about them.

Charles: What's that?

Unit 10

Table of Contents

Trash at the Beach

Have you ever gone to the beach and found plastic bags, aluminum cans, and other trash? Trash is a major cause of pollution on beaches, and in oceans, lakes, and rivers.

Trash makes beaches and water unsafe for playing and swimming. It can also be very harmful to fish. Fish can swallow plastic bags or other trash.

Many communities have special cleanup days when people pick up trash they find in and around oceans, lakes, and rivers. These volunteers provide a real service to their community because they help make the beaches and water cleaner and safer. Their work also helps fish and other organisms that live in the water. However, these good citizens must be careful, because some of the trash they pick up could be dangerous.

Buffalo Bill

In the 1870s, William F. "Buffalo Bill" Cody worked as a buffalo hunter for the railroad. His job was to kill buffalo and supply the meat to the railroad workers. Cody killed about 4,000 buffalo in 17 months.

Upon hearing stories about Buffalo Bill, people wanted to shoot buffalo themselves. Train passengers traveling the Great Plains shot the animals, just for fun, from their windows. Men known as hide hunters killed huge numbers of buffalo, skinned them, and sold the hides.

About twenty million buffalo roamed the Great Plains in the mid-1800s. By 1889, fewer than 1,000 buffalo remained. Native Americans, who relied on buffalo for food, clothing, and housing, went hungry. Some even starved. Their way of life changed forever.

Buffalo Bill and other buffalo hunters had become heroes to many. But the damage the buffalo hunters caused to Native Americans and the buffalo herds was too high a price to pay for their fame.

A Nuclear Disaster

About 1:23 a.m. on April 25, 1986, two explosions rocked the Chernobyl nuclear reactor power plant in Ukraine, a country in Eastern Europe. The shield that kept radioactive materials in the reactor flew off. Burning radioactive materials escaped and formed a large cloud. Large chunks of the burning materials started several fires. Many firefighters who battled the fires died or became very ill, as did workers at the plant. About 135,000 people had to leave their homes forever because of radioactivity.

Experts who investigated the accident said that people who worked in the plant were not trained properly. Other experts believed the nuclear reactor plant and equipment were not well designed.

We may never know if the Chernobyl accident could have been prevented. However, human error and equipment failure certainly were major causes of the disaster.

Why You Should Eat Meat

Fruits and vegetables are, without question, important parts of a healthy diet, but you also should eat meat. The main reason is simple: We are biologically built to do so.

The world is full of animal herbivores that can eat only plants. Our biological make-up is such that we are omnivores. We are able to eat and digest both plant and animal products. If we are designed to eat animals, why shouldn't we eat them?

Plus, longtime vegetarians are often advised by their doctors to eat some red meat. The human body needs iron, and red meat is the best natural source of it. Longtime vegetarians tend to be anemic and lacking in this essential mineral.

There's no ethical question anymore, either. There are many free-range farms, where livestock get to roam about and just eat all day. Who wouldn't want to do that?

Animal proteins also turn out to be the most low-fat proteins around. Nuts and cheese are very high in fat. Tofu packs more fat than chicken. There's no need to even discuss the taste difference.

It's simply a matter of the food chain. Human beings happen to be at the top of it. If you don't object to lions eating zebras, how can you object to people eating beef? It's the same thing.

Why You Should Be a Vegetarian

In the same way that you sit down to a hamburger dinner, kids in some countries dig in to meat dishes made from cats and dogs. Before you react, consider this: In some countries, there are not a lot of meat choices. Cats and dogs are seen as sources of protein rather than as pets.

If you have a problem with people eating cats and dogs, you should have the same problem with people eating cows, chickens, pigs, and fish. They're all living creatures. You probably just don't think about where your hamburger comes from.

There are many reasons to adopt a vegetarian diet. Nearly every health digest promotes fruits, vegetables, and grains for a healthy lifestyle. These foods are packed full of vitamins and minerals, things we need to fight off diseases.

In addition, there are many tasty nonanimal protein choices. Nuts, cheese, and tofu are all high in protein. You'd be pleasantly surprised by the variety of soy products that taste a lot like meat. For those of you without food allergies, these are better choices than animal proteins. Animal proteins are hard to digest.

Plus, studies have shown that the meat industry is bad for the environment. It adds to pollution and land and water shortages.

Try going vegetarian for just one week. You'll feel better and so will the animals and the entire planet.

Words of a Patriot: "We Must Be Independent!"

Boston is my home; Massachusetts is my country. And my homeland is under attack. Daily we are assaulted not with swords and cannon fire, but with taxes and intolerable acts that threaten our freedom. And who is this aggressor? England! If she has her way, all of us colonists will be taxed to death. We cannot permit that. The colonies must be free! We must be brave, fellow Patriots. We must fight for our independence! We must fight for our future!

Our grievances are many, and they are justified. Taxes are decided in London without representation of the colonies in the British Parliament. No taxes should be imposed on colonial citizens without their permission or without the vote of a representative of the colonies. No taxation without representation!

But England, thousands of miles of ocean away from us, continues to try to run the affairs of the colonies. England tramples upon our rights as free men. The way to put an end to the wrongs being done to us is to win our freedom from England. We must fight for our independence! We must fight for our future!

Boston, 1738

England says there are those in Parliament who speak for the colonies. But only representatives chosen by the colonies themselves can represent us. Even if we could elect and send a representative to Parliament in London, England is much too far away to understand our issues and respond quickly.

the Boston Tea Party of December 1773, as depicted in a color wood engraving from 1850

England says we ought to pay more in taxes to pay for its war with France—the French and Indian War, a war that is over and that England won. England says we still need protection, but the French have been defeated. We don't need protection. The truth is the war pushed England into great debt and England is taxing us to pay for the war.

Without consulting us, England has levied many taxes on the colonies. The worst was the Stamp Act, which placed a tax on almost all documents and official papers, from contracts and wills to newspapers. Even playing cards! What foolishness!

We were forced by the Tea Act to buy tea only from England, even though we could get our tea cheaper from other countries. By now you must know that some of that English tea lies on the bottom of Boston Harbor. To show our anger at this ridiculous Tea Act, some of us, disguised as Indians, dumped tea from British ships into the harbor. It was a glorious night!

Did this teach England not to place taxes upon the colonies without our consent? No. Instead, England closed Boston Harbor and outlawed our town meetings. British troops have been sent to Boston to threaten us. The troops are causing violence, not preventing it.

Colonists protest the Stamp Act of 1765.

England tells us the redcoats are here to protect us. We do not need these troops; we do not want these troops. The soldiers were shipped here to make sure the colonies do as they're told. We know that the troops are here to see to it that Boston follows the commands of a king and Parliament thousands upon thousands of miles away.

What's worse, England has forced us to keep these soldiers! We are compelled to feed them and have them sleep under our own roofs. We are given no choice in the matter, and we are given no compensation—no money to cover the cost of food and lodging for the soldiers. This is an outrageous violation of our rights to property and privacy!

England has been trying to control our rights and privileges for many years—too many years. We are convinced that the situation has gotten so bad that it is impossible to peacefully resolve the differences between England and the colonies. Fellow Patriots, the time has come for the colonies to separate from England. And we will fight, as necessary, to achieve this.

England says we are ungrateful. We are called troublemakers, traitors, and criminals. We are none of those things! We are Patriots! We come from many different backgrounds. Some of us are educated citizens and wealthy landowners. Many of us are ordinary citizens: farmers, blacksmiths, seamstresses, shopkeepers, innkeepers, and ministers. We Patriots have all come together to protect the colonies from the unreasonable dictates of England. We have come together for freedom!

a British soldier from the time of the Revolution

Words of a Patriot: "We Must Be Independent!"

**The Boston Massacre occurred on March 5, 1770.
The engraving is from the nineteenth century.**

The battle already has begun. Blood has been shed. Here in Boston, British soldiers raised their rifles and fired at people in the streets of Boston. It was a bloody massacre! This was an example of British brutality and how England believes it can do whatever it pleases. Patriots have fought British redcoats in the towns of Lexington and Concord. There were deaths and many wounded.

And yet, we will not be bullied. The time has come to stand up to English abuses. We will defy the unfair laws and taxes imposed by England. We will continue to fight to secure our freedom, now and for the future!

Citizens of the colonies, you must join Massachusetts in the struggle against tyranny!

—Patriot Josiah Wainwright

Reread the Persuasive Essay

Understand the Essay

- What is this persuasive essay about?
- What side is the writer on?
- The writer, and all Patriots, have grievances against England. Identify three.
- What is the writer's perspective of the battle occurring in Boston?
- How does the essay end?

Focus on Comprehension: Draw Conclusions

- England is using the colonies as a means to make money. How can you tell?
- England wants to maintain control over the colonies. How can you tell?
- What can you conclude about Josiah Wainwright's position on solving the problem with England?

Analyze the Tools Writers Use: State and Defend Your Position

- What position does the writer take in his essay?
- What facts and examples does the writer give to support his position?
- What emotion words does the writer use to share his opinion?

Focus on Words: Emotion Words

Below are several strong emotion words from the essay. Make a chart like the one below. Define each word and tell why the writer used it.

Page	Word	Dictionary Definition	Why is it an effective word choice?
143	intolerable		
143	tramples		
144	foolishness		
144	ridiculous		
145	outrageous		

I Saw a Ship A-Sailing

I saw a ship a-sailing,
A-sailing on the sea;
And, oh! it was all laden
With pretty things for thee!

There were comfits in the cabin
And apples in the hold;
The sails were made of silk,
And the masts were made of gold.

The four-and-twenty sailors
That stood between the decks
Were four-and-twenty white mice
With chains about their necks.

The captain was a duck
With a packet on his back;
And when the ship began to move,
The captain said, *"Quack! Quack!"*

City Kids, Country Kids (Excerpt 1)

Narrator: This is a tale about two sets of cousins. Jada, Aaron, and Olivia Sanders lived in the city. Michael and Cassie Barry lived in the country. One day, the country cousins went to visit the city cousins.

Cassie: I can't believe we're actually riding in a taxicab. And look—the buildings are so tall! I'm going to imagine we're in a boat, and the street is a river, and the buildings looming over us are the sides of a canyon. Michael, what do you think of the city so far?

Michael: I think I'm going to throw up from this bumpy cab ride.

Narrator: Meanwhile, in the city cousins' apartment . . .

Olivia: I'm so excited our cousins are coming—I can hardly sit still! It's their first time in the city, and we're going to have so much fun showing them around!

Jada: Just as long as they're not wearing overalls and straw hats.

Narrator: Soon, the two Barry children arrived.

Olivia: Hi, Michael and Cassie! Did you have any trouble finding our apartment?

Cassie: No, we just told the cab driver the address and he knew exactly where to bring us.

Michael: And he was able to find every pothole on the way, too.

Aaron: I guess it must be a big change coming to a place that has millions of people, when you're used to living isolated in the wilderness.

Michael: We don't live isolated in the wilderness! You make it sound like we're pioneers in a covered wagon.

City Kids, Country Kids (Excerpt 2)

Olivia: Jada, stop making fun of our cousins and show a little respect!

Narrator: At the skate park, the kids put on their equipment and got ready to skate.

Aaron: Try an ollie, Michael. Put your front foot over the front wheels and your back foot behind the back wheels. Then you bend your knees, and . . . pop! See?

Michael: I can do that; it looks easy. Whoops!

Narrator: The next thing Michael knew, he was on his rear end and the skateboard was rolling across the blacktop by itself.

Jada: Ha ha! *Whoom*, and down he goes!

Aaron: Michael, are you all right?

Michael: I'm fine, just get me that skateboard back— because I'm going to do it this time.

Olivia: Remember to push down with your back foot as you're lifting your front foot. See? Pop it!

Michael: Now I see what to do. Thanks. I just need to practice.

Aaron: Do you and Cassie want to try some of the small ramps?

Cassie: Not me. It looks too hard, and kind of scary.

Michael: First, I need to learn how to balance here where it's flat.

Jada: *Aw, you two are a couple of scaredy-cats. I guess that's what happens when you live in the country. You're scared of everything except hay and cows. All of you can stay here, but I'm heading over to the big half pipe.*